THE CONTENTED EXPAT
The Sequel to The Reluctant Expat

Part Two: Solar-Powered Dreams

ALAN LAYCOCK

1

Zefe, you'll be pleased to hear, recovered remarkably quickly for a man of eighty-six. His case of pleural effusion proved to be a relatively mild one and after being drip-fed antibiotics for a few days he was transferred by ambulance to Elda hospital, in order to remain under observation closer to home.

"And quite frankly because the nurses at Palencia were getting thoroughly fed up of him," Álvaro told us over lunch at our house on New Year's Day.

"Did he bore them with his stories?" Inma asked him.

"No, it wasn't that, but as he got stronger he became increasingly tactile."

"Claro," said Bernie, nodding vigorously. "Yo también... sí, yo también."

"I would also have become more tactile," I said in Spanish. "Ouch!" I added when Inma kicked me on the shin. "Hey, I was just telling Bernie what he wanted to say but couldn't because he doesn't know the subjunctive," I said in English.

"Not true," Bernie said in Spanish. "I going to say if I single old man I also tactile, but not me, as I married."

"Oh!" Cathy moaned as she clasped her head. "Can we please speak English for a while? You understand it, don't you, Álvaro?"

"Yes, if you don't speak too fast."

I smiled winningly at our neighbour, who I'd accompanied to Elda hospital several times and with whom I'd begun to converse in English, mainly to occupy his mind with something other than his ailing friend and lodger. As he'd read most of Dickens and many other books in English it didn't take him long to vocalise his extensive lexicon, although he found it quite a strain on the brain. Spending time with Álvaro was one of several New Year's resolutions that I'd made, you see, because I thought it unfair to leave him solely in the company of the old codger who I'd foisted upon him. I intended to take him out on proper walks and generally prepare him for life after Zefe, who wouldn't be around forever, despite his insistence that after his near-death experience he'd gone off the idea of kicking the bucket, or words to that effect.

My other resolutions were to find a splendid house with a well-lighted studio for my artistic wife, sell a prodigious number of solar panels and family-sized wind turbines, cover all the holidays bar Inma's at her bar, resume my coin dealing activities, continue to improve my singing, and, last but not least, learn to play tunes other than Three Blind Mice, Für Elise and Silent Night on my keyboard using both hands. You'll have noticed that flogging houses doesn't feature in my packed schedule, because I'd decided that only in the case of dire necessity would I sully my hands with any more fat envelopes. My days of being a leech on the bum of expat society were over, I truly believed.

"Alan's thinking about all the things he's going to do this year," Cathy said as she lifted the empty paella pan. "Judging by the weird faces he's pulling."

I smiled like a well-fed bishop. "Quite right, dear sister. I feel reinvigorated by our time in the north and raring to go." Álvaro's brow creased. "That means keen to get started."

"Ah, thank you."

I stood up and grasped the pan. "Allow me, Cathy. Yes, this will be a year to remember," I said, before enumerating my proposed achievements. "...although my music will be a mere pastime, of course, only to be indulged in once the day's labours are over."

"Rice is falling on the ground, Alan," said Inma.

"Ah." I grabbed the other handle. "Falling on the *floor*, yes. I shall leave the pan to soak." I did so, then filled the sink and dumped the dirty plates in it. "In our new home we'll have a dishwasher, of course, powered by the sun's rays, needless to say." I placed Cathy's strawberry cheesecake on the table and distributed plates and spoons.

"He's a proper boy scout, this one," Bernie observed.

"Seems a bit full of himself, if you ask me," said my sister.

"She means confident, or overconfident," I explained to Álvaro, whose brow told me when he hadn't understood something, as he was far too polite to interrupt.

"Ah, thank you."

"My deeds will speak for themselves," I declared. "A year from now we'll all be sitting in our new dining room." I visualised an enormous, high-ceilinged, many-windowed room containing a dining table about ten yards long. "Reflecting on 2019 and asking ourselves if we've achieved all that we set out to do." I gazed from face to face in an especially pompous manner. "What do... *you* hope to achieve this year, Bernie?"

He raised his hands then clasped them on the table. "Us farmers pray for good weather and hope that our backbreaking toil will be rewarded. We don't make rash resolutions, but simply observe the passing of the seasons and soldier on through the sunshine and the rain, the heat and the cold, living out our humble lives and hoping that God will grant us abundant harvests."

"Amen," I said.

Cathy shook her head. "What a pair." Her eyes narrowed as they met mine. "And of course you won't have to worry about your humble allotment, seeing as you'll be upping sticks at some point."

As Álvaro had kept our little plot in tiptop shape and I'd recently given it a quick going over with the hoe, I was able to assert that I intended to stay on top of it until the eleventh hour. "Or even the twelfth, because Liz and Ben won't want to encounter a mass of weeds when they move in."

"I will help," said Álvaro. "For me it is therapeutic to do a little work, away from my house."

"Yes, I bet it is. Do you have, er… any res–"

"Álvaro isn't in a position to make fanciful resolutions like you," Inma said rapidly in Spanish. "Not with Zefe in his house," she added in English. "Isn't that so, Álvaro?"

He smiled stoically. "Like Bernie, I will… soldier on. I choose… chose to invite Zeferino to my home, so I will care for him." He shrugged. "Before Zefe I had only my books. Since then I have a companion to speak with of ideas and history and stories. I cannot complain."

Just then I pictured the two of us in a lawyer's office, being told that Zefe had left us all his worldly goods. I shook my head to dispel this avaricious and totally unsummoned scene.

"You must ask the town council for assistance," said Inma.

Álvaro sighed. "Oh, no, he detests all official helpers."

"That's why I stepped in, if you remember," I said.

"And quickly passed the buck," said Cathy.

"Not so quickly," I muttered.

"Which book is this?" said Álvaro.

Bernie guffawed. "Nice one, Alv."

I explained the expression and Álvaro immediately absolved me, before beginning to relate Zefe's latest near-death-experience yarn. "Yesterday he told me that he was flying above the gold mine where he once worked in Brazil. In that huge open mine there were thousands of men, small groups working each portion. Zefe was floating above, then saw something shining, so he fly… flew down and took a big piece of gold, but when flying up again he realise that it is useless to a dead man, so he drops it and hundreds of men start to fight for it." He shrugged. "That is about the ten… tenth near-death story that he tells me."

"I've heard a couple," I said. "But he hasn't explained how he had so many."

Álvaro tittered. "Easy. He says he was near death for many, many hours, so many things happened to him."

"You don't think he really was in Brazil, do you? I mean, I read about that Sierra Pelada mine later and it's true that all sorts of people went there to try to make their fortunes. Not only miners, but teachers and doctors and… well, it sounded like a genuine gold rush. I know his story about hacking his way through the jungle with his gold was nonsense, but could he have flown to Brazil and joined the gold-diggers?"

Álvaro shrugged. "In theory he has told me the true story of his life. In it he mentioned Detroit and Caracas, but not Brazil."

"In the version he told me he didn't mention Caracas, so he might not have told either of us about Brazil."

"It's possible, but I doubt it."

"Why so much interest in this gold-mining business, mate?" said Bernie.

I swallowed a bit of cheesecake and cleared my throat. "As you're my nearest and dearest I'll confess that thoughts regarding

Zefe's inheritance are apt to cross my mind from time to time. During his recent trip to the lawyer's I feel sure that he made Álvaro his main beneficiary, but also left me something. These may be unworthy and greedy thoughts, but I can't help having them."

Inma patted my hand. "You're only human, Alan."

"When was this gold rush?" said Bernie, phone in hand.

"I think a farmer found the first bit of gold in seventy-nine, but please read about it later. If I see those photos of the swarming miners again I'll have gold on the brain when Zefe comes home."

Bernie promptly disobeyed me and his eyes darted down the screen. "Bloody hell, then someone found a lump that weighed nearly *seven* kilos. They'd started pouring in by then, but I guess there'd have been flights to Rio from Madrid or Lisbon, so he could have got there pretty quick and it's only… let's see, oh, a hell of a long way to the mine. Still, it was doable."

"Another smartphone addict," I grumbled, before swallowing the saliva which had somehow begun to fill my mouth without the aid of cheesecake.

"It's my phone," said Cathy, and whisked it away.

"Aw!"

I rubbed my hands together. "Anyway, enough fantasising. When Zefe gets home I'll help you out a bit more than before, Álvaro, because it isn't fair to leave everything to you."

Bernie looked wistfully at the phone. "I'll drive over and keep him company too, as I'm not so busy on my land right now. Hey, maybe he could come to ours for a change of scene."

Cathy looked at Inma and shook her head. "Gold fever."

"Yes."

"Well, he did once tell me that he was wealthier than his scruffy old flat suggested," I said.

Álvaro nodded. "To me too. I sometimes ask myself if he really lost all his money in the casino in Caracas." He slapped the table. "Oh, enough speculation. It makes no difference to me. I will drive to Elda later and I hope they tell me when he can come home."

"I'll come along," I said.

Bernie grinned. "Me too."

I frowned. "I've been three times, before this silly gold speculation began."

"I was joking. What's yours is mine anyway, and you still owe me sixteen years' back rent."

"But I... I..."

"Shut up, you two," said Cathy. "How is Zefe behaving with the nurses at Elda hospital, Álvaro?"

He smiled. "After the first day, quite well. His principal nurses are now two large individuals called Jose and Pablo. He is not tactile with them, but tells them stories."

"Near-death stories?" I asked.

"No, all the old ones that you and I know well, but with new, er... tergiversaciones."

"Twists," said Cathy, vocabulary being her strongest linguistic suit.

I nodded. "I knew that."

"Me too," said Bernie.

"Balls."

"Cojones."

"Yes, the old stories with new twists," said Álvaro. "Ah, yes, his mind is still very alive, and as he has decided to live I expect he will live long. I hope so, anyway. I sometimes complain, but he is good company for me, on the whole."

Inma stood up to collect the cheesecake plates. "Let us speak of something else now."

"Yes," said Cathy. "So how sure are you that Liz and Ben will buy the house?"

I told her that during their recent visit they'd shown no signs of getting cold feet. "In fact they're keener than ever, so I intend to start scouting the area for our dream home right away, before I begin to sell solar gear about a fortnight from now."

"Will you ask at the other estate agents, or just rely on Juanca?" said Bernie.

I smiled. "Tomorrow I'm going window shopping with Juan." I stood up. "I'll make the coffee."

"He's leaving us to mull over his enigmatic statement," said Cathy.

Álvaro stroked his slightly pointy beard. "Windows?"

Bernie sniggered. "They'll go round the estate agents looking in the windows and Juan will tell him where the houses are."

I grinned. "Yes, and I'll take photos of any good ones that he can't place. Someone in Vicente's bar is bound to know where they are."

"He doesn't want anyone else to get a fat envelope, you see," Inma said from the kitchen area.

"That's right. I intend to cut out those parasitic middlemen and contact the owners directly. Bernie, do you remember when you posed as a customer to get the lowdown on what Angela and Malcolm might want to buy?"

"Yeah, I enjoyed that."

"And you found their future hotel."

He ran his hand over his bronzed bonce. "Sure did."

"So I may ask you to do it again, looking for an old house or a chalet without a pool this time."

"OK, but why without a pool?"

"Because we want the best possible house with a bit of land for a maximum of €150,000. All these expats who come here can't live without a pool, but we're above such needless luxuries."

"I'm not," Inma said.

"For now. We can always have one built later. A ten-thousand-euro pool and a pretty patio can add thirty grand to the price of a property, so I shan't be falling for that little ruse, oh no."

Inma yawned theatrically.

I rubbed my hands together. "Oh, yes, somewhere around here there's a lovely house with our name on it, and I mean to find it very soon. Liz and Ben can pay for this place right away, so come the spring I expect to be installed in our new home, strolling around our not too extensive grounds."

"While I look out of our lovely big windows, one after the other," Inma said from the dingy kitchen.

Over coffee Álvaro insisted on going to visit Zefe alone, not wishing to break up our family gathering. As our gold fever had subsided by then I handed him the keys to my Clio and told him I'd accompany him the following afternoon. As I mentioned in my first book, in Spain a relative is expected to sleep over with the patient in hospital, partly to attend to their nightly needs, but mainly due to tradition, as in the past most folk who entered a ward weren't all that likely to leave it alive. Álvaro had done this once back in Palencia, but Zefe had proved so tiresome that he hadn't repeated the experience, partly so that the patient would get more sleep, but mainly to conserve his own mental wellbeing.

So, after a tiny glass of cava he left us to polish off the bottle. Imagine our surprise when about an hour and a half later he knocked and entered.

"The ambulance is about to arrive," he said in Spanish.

"Who for?" said a slightly tipsy Bernie.

"With Zefe. I offered to drive him home, but they insisted on finishing their onerous job correctly."

I laughed at his witticism.

"The doctor's words, not mine. He told me that during twenty-two years at the hospital he has only had one patient more troublesome than Zefe."

"Quién?" Bernie asked him.

"A circus clown who went off his head. He rushed from ward to ward, acting the clown and endangering the lives of the more afflicted patients."

"And Zefe also rush from ward to ward?" Cathy asked in Spanish.

"No, from the comfort of his bed he summoned the staff constantly, for one trivial reason or another." He shook his head sadly. "And he was always so well-behaved when I was there. Oh, well, I'd better go and meet them."

"We all go," said Bernie.

"We *will* all go," I said.

"Whatever."

While descending the track we saw a hefty orderly impatiently ordering Zefe out of the ambulance, but only when his audience had arrived did he deign to step down, using both of his sticks. He looked a little pale, but his eyes flashed as wickedly as ever.

"Thanks for fetching him," I said to the youngish chap.

He nodded. "Who's looking after him?"

Álvaro raised his hand.

"Good luck, amigo," he said, before jumping in and banging the door shut behind him. The ambulance raised a good deal of dust before reaching the nearby road.

"They must have an urgent case," said Bernie.

"Or an urgent desire to leave here."

I felt the tip of a walking stick pressing into the small of my back. "Hey, I've only just come back and you're already ignoring me, you rotten bast... people."

"Cómo estás, Zefe?" said Cathy.

"Bah, I could have been home for Christmas." He pointed the other stick at Álvaro. "But this one conspired to keep me locked up. I told that lot in Elda that I'd flown in the face of death and that death had retreated, but they just kept stuffing me with bloody pills." He approached me, but instead of taking the proffered hand, he wrinkled his mottled nose. "You've been drinking."

"Oh, just a glass of cava."

He pointed a stick up the track. "Lead me to it."

"Can you walk up there?"

"Course I can." He began to shuffle along. "This morning I walked around all the rooms on my floor, telling everybody I was leaving."

"Apparently this eventful little tour led to the doctor taking the decision to discharge him," Álvaro murmured in Spanish. "He said that although it was a little soon, he had to take into account the overall welfare of his patients and staff."

Zefe paused. "Already gossiping about me, eh? God, I'm thirsty."

"Er, remember what the specialist said about alcohol, Zeferino," said the only person who still occasionally used his full name.

He dug his sticks into the ground and leered over his shoulder. "I don't give a toss what that young trollop said," he barked, or words very much to that effect. "Doctor García's the only one who I'll pay attention to. *He* knows his job." He plodded on. "You can start filling my glass."

Álvaro stayed put and wiped his glasses with a large handkerchief. "Oh dear, the doctor's throwaway comment is now forever etched on the old devil's mind."

"I heard that!"

"What comment?" I said.

"On the subject of alcohol. While the specialist forbade him to drink it, Doctor García said he was such a tough old bird that a little wine would do him no harm."

"Hmm, like a red… wine label to a bull, eh?"

"Cómo?"

I explained the original expression.

"Exactly."

"You must ration him to two small glasses a day, Álvaro."

"Easier said than done."

"Keep the wine at our house, if you like."

He chuckled. "All right, if you wish to receive several visits a day."

"Ah." After Zefe's first vulgar outburst Cathy and Inma had chosen a more circuitous route back to the house, as my wife didn't really have much time for the foul-mouthed old brute, and it appeared that Bernie had felt obliged to join them. "Maybe not then. You'll just have to be tough with him."

"Oh, I try, I really do."

When we reached the gate Zefe's nose was already about an inch from the door.

"Come on, come on! I haven't had a drink since I caught that chill in Palencia."

I grasped Álvaro's arm. "I'm going to try something. He often reacts better to barbarities than to sensible advice."

I squeezed past the impatient oldster and opened the unlocked door, before ushering him to the chair at the head of the table. He grabbed both of the empty cava bottles and shook them.

"Bah, not a drop! What can a man get to drink in this dingy place?"

"One moment, Zefe."

I rinsed and dried a traditional pint glass I'd bought for Bernie but which he'd never used.

"Is this big enough?"

He grinned and banged his fists on the table. "Depends on what you're going to put in it, ha ha."

I then beckoned Álvaro through to a little pantry in the cave proper where we kept our store of booze which consisted mostly of unwanted presents.

"Take these two and I'll grab these."

"Er, are you sure about this, Alan?"

"Yes, I think so. It'll be a form of shock therapy."

"The ladies are going to get a shock when they see it."

"Come on."

We stomped in and arranged a semi-circle of bottles around his glass. "Right, Zefe, you've got whisky, brandy, gin, vodka and, er… herb liqueur. Which is it to be first?"

He grinned and rubbed his hands together, but his eyes revealed the confusion he felt.

I screwed the top off the JB bottle. "How about whisky, so you can relive that lovely night in Palencia?"

His head moved back an inch or so.

"Want to sniff it? No? How about a glass of vodka then, to recall your days in Leningrad? Or maybe a brandy or some of this herby stuff."

I felt tempted to slosh a hideous mixture into his glass, but his nonplussed expression made me desist.

"What's this all about, Alan?" he murmured.

"On stepping out of the ambulance after almost two weeks in hospital you demanded a drink, so here it is. If you have a death wish we might as well get it over with sooner rather than later."

He turned the whisky bottle so that the label faced the other way. "Don't be silly, Alan. I only fancied a little glass of cava to celebrate the new year with my friends."

Noting a hint of moisture in his beady eyes, I feared I'd upset him. He grasped his right-hand stick with both hands and leant over it, trying to hide his face, I presumed.

"Well, maybe my joke was a little harsh," I mumbled as I leant over to reach for the bottles.

He then whacked me on the arse with the stick.

"Ow!"

"Fuck me!" said Bernie from the doorway. "Ouch!" he added on receiving a cuff from Cathy.

She eyed the table display, then watched me rubbing my bum. "What in God's name is going on here?"

"I…"

"Shock treatment," said Álvaro.

"Your brother wants to murder me," Zefe wailed with delight.

"Please explain this, Alan," said my wife.

While Álvaro returned the bottles to their rightful place, I explained that Zefe never responded to gentle persuasion and that I'd succeeded in freaking him out by overwhelming him with booze.

I patted the feisty old rogue on the head. "And now he's cured."

He nodded. "I will be after a tiny glass of wine, for the nerves, you know."

Between dainty sips he told us how the night before he'd dreamt that he was walking through a tunnel at the end of which the light became increasingly brighter. "Then I emerged into a luscious glade where – and you may not believe this – I found myself face to face with my younger self. 'Hello, young Zeferino,' I said to the handsome and powerfully built man of thirty. 'Hello, old Zefe,' he replied with a smile. 'Walk this way,' he said, so I did, and he also walked towards me. I thought he was going to kiss me, but when his lips reached my face I was temporarily blinded and felt an immense pressure on my chest. When I recovered my sight a short time later I was alone in the glade." He sipped.

"Then what?" said Bernie.

"I woke up." He gazed from face to face. "What do you think it means?"

It means that you've spun a yarn in which we're to believe that your younger self entered your body and restored some of your former strength, I thought but didn't say. "It's a real mystery," I said.

"Do you think that happened in Brazil?" Bernie asked him.

"Eh?" Zefe's eyes opened wide, then narrowed. "Why do you ask me that, young man?"

"Oh, because I believe... eek! Why are you squeezing my leg, Alan?"

"Zefe mustn't tire himself out," I muttered.

I groaned inwardly as Zefe polished off his wine, wiped his mouth, and grinned at each of us in turn. "So, you've been discussing my mining adventure in the Sierra Pelada, have you? I wonder why."

"Álvaro and I were recalling several of your escapades, not only that one," I said.

He sniggered. "Yes, yes, while the old man lies languishing in hospital, his friends ponder on the true outcome of his daring trip into the Brazilian hinterland."

"We mentioned France, Norway and Finland too."

"Liar. Brazil is the trip that you two hyenas rack your brains about. Did he really go? Did he get lucky? Was he able to return with his stash intact?" He pointed at Álvaro. "As you sat by my bedside while I fought for my life, I could see a golden hue in your apparently sorrowful eyes, and as for you, you big lanky guiri, you've been after my money ever since the day you walked into my flat and began to turn my life upside down."

Cathy snorted and Inma growled.

"Don't worry," said Álvaro, unfazed by his seemingly venomous attack. "This is all part of our ongoing game."

"It's a shame we've missed the poisonous mushrooms this year," I said as I scowled at the old reprobate.

He cackled. "Yes, you missed your chance again, and as I have to visit the damned local doctor every week I'll be able to tell her if you try anything else, so instead of dancing on my grave you'll end up rotting in jail, the pair of you."

Inma's chair scraped as she stood up. "I'm going to dig up some potatoes."

"I'll come with you," said Cathy. They left.

"More wine!" Zefe cried.

"No," I said.

"That's a pity. I was going to tell you the true story of Brazil, but with a dry mouth I'll be unable to do so."

I began to rise, but changed my mind. "Sorry, Zefe, but you can't have any more. We wish to keep you alive for the time being."

"Another drop won't hurt him," said Bernie, who was far less familiar with his wily ways.

"My story about escaping through the jungle and rowing up the river to Belém was a lot of nonsense, of course, but the actual mining…" He stuck out his tongue and coughed in a grotesque manner. "No, it's no good… too dry," he whined hoarsely.

I grabbed the white wine bottle from the fridge and poured half an inch into his glass. "And this is only because Bernie's here."

He sipped, then told us a perfectly feasible tale about how he'd flown to Caracas, looked up his old friends, then assembled a prospecting team which flew first to French Guiana, then chartered a small plane to Marabá. "A mere hundred and fifty kilometres from the mine but, oh, how difficult it was to complete that final leg! It was the spring of 1980 and men were still arriving by the hundreds every day. We eventually got a farmer to drive us there in his truck, but do you know how much he charged us?"

"How much?" said that sucker Bernie, who was lapping it up, the ingenuous chump.

"Five hundred American dollars, the rogue. From there we had a long walk to the mine, where we bought materials to build a shack. The next day we were granted a small plot in the furthermost area of the mine, so we went down the enormous ladders and set to work. By then the days of the huge lumps of gold were over, but we dug and sieved diligently for a month until we were only finding the tiniest specks of gold dust." He yawned. "Oh, Álvaro, you'd better take me home now. I feel very tired all of a sudden."

My indulgent chuckle did nothing to reduce the size of Bernie's eyes, which appeared to be close to popping out of their sockets. "So how well you do, Zefe?"

He yawned. "Oh, as I say, the days of vast fortunes were practically over by then, but the five of us all felt reasonably pleased with our earnings, although of course the expenses had been high too." This time his yawn was so vast that his upper teeth became detached from his gum. "Oh, so sleepy."

Álvaro chuckled. "Your time in hospital has tired you out. Now you must have a few quiet days."

He yawned in agreement, before the three of us accompanied him slowly down the track.

"Bye for now, Zefe," I said at the door. "Try not to be too much of a pain in the arse."

"Zefe, one day I can pick you up and…" Bernie felt my left foot upon his right one. "Why do you keep assaulting me today, Alan?"

"Come on, let's get back."

In the fading light we strolled up to join the spud diggers.

"Ah, just look at nature's subterranean bounty," I enthused. "You've missed one there, Inma."

She wiped her forehead with the back of her grubby hand. "Gracias, Señor."

"Oh!" Bernie wailed, before slapping his cheeks several times.

"What's up?"

He pointed at the churned up earth. "I thought I saw a lump of gold, but it was just another spud."

"Bernie, you must take everything that Zefe says with a pinch of gold dust, and I mean everything. You've heard a few of his stories and know how convincing he can be. Now he thinks he's onto a winner with this gold mining business."

"It'll be a lot of nonsense," said Cathy.

"Silly old man," said Inma.

Bernie steered me away from the sneering females. "Don't you think there could be an ounce of gol… truth in his story though?"

"No." I thought about the Caracas connection and his team's prosaic achievements. "I'm almost sure it's a pack of lies."

"Yeah, I suppose so. Be nice to him though, just in case."

"I will."

2

"That woman with blue hair just gave you an evil stare," Juan said the next morning as I took a shot of a chalet in an estate agent's window display.

"I don't care." I snapped a large white house priced at €195,000. "She's the, er... arregladora," I said, meaning 'fixer', I hoped.

"The what?"

I led him away from her accusing eyes. "The woman who took control of our affairs when we first arrived here and attempted to steer us towards the expat scene, so that we'd never learn the language and would always require her services. Ha, I soon put paid to that by meeting you guys and learning Spanish in a matter of weeks."

He sniggered. "You spoke like an especially stupid Hollywood Indian for a long, long time, Alan, before your phrases began to make more sense. Isn't that last house you photographed way beyond your budget?"

"Who knows? It depends how much these vultures mean to keep for themselves."

"Yes, well, you'll know all about that. Diego was asking after you. Cristóbal is still short of work and hopes that you'll find him some more soon."

I sighed. "Then you must break the news to him that I've retired from that line of work. On the other hand, if any of his customers need solar panels, I'm the man to ask, or soon will be."

He led me to a bench in a small paved square and we sat down facing the mild sun.

"The thing is, Juan…"

He raised his beefy hand. "I know all about your qualms regarding house sales, Alan, so you don't need to repeat them yet again, but don't you feel a sense of solidarity with your fellow men?"

"Which men?"

"Cristóbal and his workers, almost all of whom have families to support. With this solar panel business you'll be coming into contact with a lot of fellow guir… foreigners, so it would cost you nothing to put Cristóbal forward as the best builder around."

"Oh, I'll still do that, out of the goodness of my heart, tell him." I looked at my watch. "Hmm, almost eleven. In a moment we'll go to Juanca's and see what he's got in his window display."

Juan gasped. "That greedy devil will probably have a fit if he sees you photographing his wares. Has your heart suddenly turned to stone or something?"

I grinned. "He won't see me, thanks to you."

"Eh?"

I stood up. "Come on, he'll be crossing the road to the bar right now. You're to go for a coffee and make sure he doesn't look across the street. It won't take me a minute, then I'll join you."

He shook his big bald head. "I ask myself who is the bigger rogue, you or him."

"Him. Thanks, Juan."

"Oh, it passes the time."

During our days of more or less harmonious collaboration I'd managed to persuade Juanca to have some semblance of a display in his windows, rather than keeping the properties hidden away in his file for fear of other estate agents filching them, as he was wont to do with theirs. I now saw that he'd regressed to his secretive old ways and was only displaying photos of some 'new' flats in a block built just before the crash of 2008, a couple of ruins, and a few plots of land. Short of breaking in and rifling through his file, the next best solution would be to invent a potential buyer who was looking for a 150K dwelling without a pool, but my lofty moral standards didn't permit me to stoop quite so low. I elected to test the water before deciding how to proceed, because I'd only seen a couple of appealing properties in the other agencies and it was sod's law that Juanca would hold the key to our dream home.

"Alan! Happy New Year!" the tubby trader bellowed, before pumping my hand and telling the owner to grant me my heart's desire.

"Un cortado descafeinado, por favor. Hola, Juanca, feliz año."

"What a surprise to see you two here."

"How's business?" I asked.

He swiped his cares away. "Oh, never mind that. It's so good to see you! How was the rest of your stay in the north? How's Inma?" He remembered Juan's presence. "How's your good wife Marta?"

"Bien," said Juan.

"Inma's fine. The north was good. How are things with you?"

His cheek muscles slackened. "Oh, business is slow."

"I meant at home and... things."

He sighed. "My wife has come back. She decided that a life of poverty with that insignificant man wasn't for her, so we've made our peace, more or less."

I smiled. "Didn't you fear that she'd get half your riches?"

His smile dwarfed mine. "I did fear that at one point, yes, but suddenly most of my assets disappeared."

"What do you mean?"

He shrugged. "Oh, my financial advisor and I put our heads together and before long I only had the house, which had become heavily remortgaged for reasons known only to ourselves. When her lawyer pointed out that she was married to a kind of financial Houdini, she began to see the error of her ways, as by the time she got her hands on anything we'd probably both be ancient or dead."

"It doesn't sound like a very satisfactory reconciliation. Oh, and what happened to the pretty woman you brought to our wedding party?" I said, realising that I hadn't asked him a thing about his personal life for ages.

"Oh, she was just a… a friend who I persuaded to come with me. The wife and I get along all right. All I ask is that my clothes are pressed and my meals upon the table. I'm able to satisfy my other needs elsewhere," he said, glancing slyly at Juan.

"Claro," said he with a gravelly chuckle.

"Er, am I missing something here?"

Juan smiled. "You're missing nothing, because you have Inma."

"Hmm… oh, I see, I think." I frowned at Juanca. "You mean you go to those roadside hotels when you wish to satisfy certain needs?" I said, referring to the puticlubs, aka brothels.

He shrugged. "Occasionally."

"And you, Juan?"

His mouth fell open and he pointed at himself. "Me? Of course not. I wouldn't set foot in those sinful places."

"Good."

"I haven't been for years. Right, I'll leave you to it, as you'll wish to talk shop."

"No, I… we…" I began, but he was off.

"How are things up at the cave?" Juanca asked me.

"Good." I took a deep breath, then exhaled slowly through my nostrils. "But we're selling it to that couple who came, Liz and Ben."

He nodded placidly. "Yes, I know."

"Ah, I… what? How the devil do you know that?"

"Oh, yesterday I made a few courtesy calls. I saw their number and thought I might as well wish them luck for the coming year."

"Yes, well, that's partly why I've come to see you today," I improvised. "They loved the place and Inma finds it dingy, so… well, that's what's going to happen."

He chuckled and patted me on the back. "You don't need to excuse yourself, Alan."

"I know."

"I'm happy for them, if that's what they want."

"Yes, me too."

"Because I'm not obsessed with making money."

"No."

"Which is just as well, as I'm making very little right now."

"Ah."

"Another coffee?"

"No, gracias."

"So, I expect you'll need to look for another house."

"Er, yes, that's the idea."

He smiled. "You'll find nothing of interest in my window."

"No." I rubbed the back of my head, suspecting that he had eyes in the back of his.

He chuckled. "Now I'm going to guess what type of house you're looking for."

"Go on then."

"Well, bearing in mind the excellent price you're getting for the cave house…"

"Ha… han… hang on a minute. You're not telling me they just happened to mention that while you were exchanging season's greetings?"

"No, no, I light-heartedly hazarded a guess at the price and proved to be wrong by only five thousand."

"I see."

"I guessed 140,000, you see, in case you hadn't agreed on a price, as I wished them to believe the property was worth so much, which we both know it isn't, but I have your best interests at heart."

"Gracias."

"Now, back to your future home. You and Inma aren't the types who foolishly wish to spend their last peseta on a house, and you, Alan, are always eager to distance yourself from your fellow foreigners, so my guess is that you'll wish to spend up to 150,000 on an older house without a pool, because we both know how essential pools are to your compatriots."

I shook my head and smiled. "And how much land will we want with the house?"

He stroked his smooth chin. "Hmm, let me see. The house will have to be detached, of course, as you're used to that, but after your inertia regarding those dead almond trees, I believe you'd prefer to have only a small amount of land, as you aren't an aspiring farmer like your brother-in-law."

"Ha, next you'll tell me that you called them yesterday too."

"Yes, in the evening. Bernie insisted on addressing me in Castilian and said something rather incoherent about gold for some reason. Anyway, I have… but no, we shan't speak about business today."

"Spit it out."

He patted his lips. "What?"

"Tell me about the perfect house that you've already found for us."

"Ha, what house? I've just had three whole days' holiday and scarcely remember what I have in my file."

"Claro."

"Anyway, as you didn't contact me after coming to an agreement with your buyers shortly after our fruitless house hunting trip, I assume you wish to go it alone and contact the owners directly."

I stiffened my spine. "Yes, that's right."

"And why not? You now have the know-how, after all, don't you?"

"Yes."

"And you've already seen what the other agencies have to offer, due to their foolish transparency."

I threw my hands to my head. "Oh, this is too much! How the hell do you know that?"

He grinned. "Do you remember Sandra?"

"Yes, I've just seen her."

"And she's just seen you, so she called me to say that you'd been snooping around taking photos."

"I thought you wanted nothing to do with her."

"Alan, in my game – or should I say our game? – it's sometimes expedient to ally oneself with those with whom one feels little affinity. She now works at the estate agency where you saw her, but as she's an avaricious little witch she's been known to liaise with me from time to time." He sighed. "And as you will now no doubt tell me once again that you no longer wish to sully your hands with filthy commissions, I have little choice but to work with less appealing people, like her." Another sigh. "Ah, such is my lot, despite spreading happiness for so many years."

"I suppose you know I'm going to be selling solar panels."

"Of course. Say nothing in your friend Vicente's bar which you don't wish to become common knowledge within the week. Regarding that venture, I foresee a fruitful collaboration between us."

"Do you?"

"Of course. You'll see that for yourself once you've begun. Right, since you're here we may as well go and take a look at my file."

"All right," I said, feeling slightly demoralised by his apparent omnipotence, or at least omnipresence.

Juanca's fat file contained all the houses I'd photographed – estate agents in Spain don't usually have exclusive selling rights to properties – plus another three which were new to me.

"How come none of the other agencies have these?"

"This pretty chalet to the north of here belongs to a British couple. I sold them the house seven years ago and they were so happy with my work that they want me and me alone to sell it for them. This older house on the edge of a hamlet belongs to an elderly Spanish couple who wish to move to town. They also hold me in high esteem, because several years ago I got a good price for some land which they sold. You see, Alan, due to my reputation I have almost every desirable property in my file, unlike that pack of amateurs you chose to visit first."

"Yes, Juanca. I don't like the chalet much, and this one's too far from Inma's bar."

"Which leaves this fine two-storey place set in a modest olive grove. Ha, your brother-in-law would be delighted to care for the trees, I'm sure, and it isn't *too* far from his house."

"Yes, I've seen it on my bike rides," I lied. "I quite like the look of it." I turned over the page. "Where's the price?"

He smiled. "In my head."

"And do you and you alone have the right to sell it?"

"Ah, yes, well, this is a rather different case, you see."

"How?"

"Well, over the years so many people have enquired about the house, due to its fine facade and imposing position at the foot of the wooded sierra, that I visited the owners some time ago. The couple had no desire to sell their lovely home, but we had a pleasant chat and I ordered some furniture."

"You what?"

He shrugged. "They own a furniture shop in Elche, quite a way away, as you know. They told me their son and daughter lived down there and they had two grandchildren who they didn't see as often as they wished. She sometimes felt lonely in the house and lamented not being closer to their loved ones. It was then that I perused the catalogue more thoroughly and ordered a small chest of drawers and two bedside tables. Before leaving I asked permission to take pictures of the house, me being a keen photographer, and we parted on extremely friendly terms."

My eyes narrowed. "Did you, er... tell them you were an estate agent?"

He smiled. "No, I think that slipped my mind. I was out walking you see, me being a keen hiker."

"Yeah, right," I said in English.

"And on seeing the man outside I stopped to pass the time of day." He patted the sheet of photos. "Anyway, they're in their sixties and will probably retire soon. Then the pull of the grandchildren will really assert itself and should they get a good offer for the house they might consider selling up and moving closer to Elche, or so my almost infallible instinct tells me."

I stood up and paced around, shaking my head. "Do you often do that kind of thing?"

"No, no often. Only when I get an overpowering urge to follow my nose."

"It seems a bit intrusive to me, not to say deceptive."

"But what can I do? Selling houses is my vocation and the owners don't always know what's best for them. No doubt they expected their family to visit more often, but people are busy these days and many prefer the beach in summer. I suspect that if a pleasant friend of mine, you for instance, were to offer them... oh, €170,000 or so, partly in cash, they might see the light. He's rather stubborn, you see, and wouldn't deign to put his house up for sale, but were a fortuitous opportunity to arise..."

I shook my head. "It's underhand, and too expensive anyway."

"It's a marvellous investment and a lovely house." He slapped his thighs and rubbed his tummy. "I need to get more exercise. How about you and I going for a walk this weekend?"

I looked at an especially nice photo of the white house in which its green window shutters almost matched the olive trees and the pine woods beyond. I sighed. "It's true that you seldom see houses like this for sale."

"No, people love such places and hate to contemplate parting with them, and when they do they never stay on the market for long. Imagine, they were prepared to commute so far every day in order to live in such a verdant place, compared to Elche anyway, a veritable desert, although its 200,000 palm trees do have a certain charm. Hmm, yes, I'll remember to mention the palm trees when we call in on Saturday, or shall we make it Sunday?"

I shrugged. "I suppose Inma might like to do a little painting around there."

He clapped. "Oh, yes, painting. A perfect alib... reason to visit that curious oasis."

An oasis which I can't quite place, I thought. "No, not only is your projected price too expensive, but I think the house is too far from Inma's bar."

"Bah, no further away than you are now."

"Well, I suppose we could... oh, no, no, we couldn't."

"What?"

"When I tell Inma the circumstances of our sneaky visit she won't hear of it." On smoothing back my hair I remembered I had a mind of my own underneath it. "And nor will I. It's... it's preposterous. You've no right to interfere. You must leave them in peace."

"Yes, yes, leave them to rot among their olive trees while their grandchildren frolic under the palmeras ilicitanas (Elche's palm trees). Due to the man's stubbornness, his wife will pine away in the shadow of the pines, while life's great tapestry is woven elsewhere."

"Save your eloquence, Juanca. I daren't tell Inma that I'd even considered this Machiavellian proposal."

He shrugged. "Muy bien."

I slipped the sheet back into the file.

"You and I will have to go walking alone then."

I retrieved the sheet. "All right, but only because I want to see how far your fat little legs will carry you."

"Ha, ha, that's the spirit."

"Saturday then, as Inma's working in the morning."

"OK."

Then something crucial occurred to me which had completely slipped my mind. "Er, Juanca, in the extremely unlikely case that they wish to sell, and if I approve of their reasons for selling, and if we like the house, and if we can afford it, how much do you hope to make from the transaction?"

He clasped his heart and gasped.

I eyed the discoloured ceiling. "Spare me the theatricals, sinvergüenza (shameless one)."

He slumped onto a chair and undid the second button of his lime-green shirt, before wafting his face with the only sheet in his file which interested me.

"Well? How much?"

"Oh, Alan, do you really believe that after all the successful deals we've pulled off together I would contemplate making a profit from this one?"

"Yes."

More wafting. "You do me an injustice, my friend, and do you know why?"

I sighed. "Why?"

He slapped down the sheet and jumped up, so I sat down in the other chair. He began to pace around with his hands clasped behind his back. "You're no fool, Alan, despite what some people say, so I won't pretend that there haven't been times when I would have gladly taken a chunk from any sale I arranged for you, such as when you—"

"Stop right there! Cristóbal cut you out of the hotel refurbishment deal, not me," I interjected to save time. "Please get to the point."

"All right. I'll find you a superb house out of the goodness of my heart, despite losing what I could make by selling it to someone else, for two reasons. Firstly because I'm fond of you, and Inma too, and secondly because our working lives are far from over. I foresee years of collaboration between us, and although during my career people have called me many things, short-sighted isn't one of them. Now, before you play your usual scratched record about commissions, I'll tell you that these solar panels and whatnot are the key to our future success."

"Yes, you said."

"Having an ally flogging that gear around here will be a godsend to me."

"Hmm, I sort of see why, but… but not exactly."

"Oh, we're all little spiders on this tangled property web and must help each other. You'll be out and about, up and down, here and there, touting your wares and talking to the foreigners."

"And Spaniards too. The whole area is to be exclusively mine."

He came to an abrupt halt. "Really?"

I smiled. "Oh, yes, I insisted on that."

"Have you, er… ever sold anything to a Spaniard?"

"No, but what difference does it make who they are?" I stood up and he sat down. "I'll have top-notch products at competitive prices at a time when the economy is looking up and people are more aware than ever before how important it is to protect the environment." I paced around with my hands aloft. "I've chosen exactly the right moment to become involved in this sector," I said, hoping he didn't know how I'd met my boss. "People are beginning to buy electric cars and generally becoming attuned to what the future holds for them, and now that the reactionary Partido Popular are out and the forward-thinking socialists are in, there are more grants for alternative energy and… things like that."

He smiled. "Have you been rehearsing?"

"No, well, a little bit in my head. If you think I can't sell to Spaniards you underestimate me."

"Yes, well, visit a few foreigners first. Bernie will be able to advise you how to approach them. Then when you've seen a couple of Spaniards you can come to me and I'll tell you where you went wrong and how you ought to approach them."

"Bah, we're all Europeans."

"Yes, well, some say that Europe begins at the Pyrenees, or ends there, depending on where they are. As for you British, well, we've seen how European you lot are."

I shook a forefinger at him. "All the Brits who live in Spain voted to stay in the EU, apart from a few flag-waving, beer-guzzling half-wits who must be living in such... befuddled isolation that they don't even know where they are," I ranted, more or less.

Juanca had become pensive. "Hmm, so you'll need another adviser too."

"What? Who?"

"You seem to know your countrymen, and I know mine, but there are Germans, Dutch, French and all sorts coming to live around here nowadays. Another approach will be required with true Europeans, I imagine, but we'll cross that bridge when you come to it. Right, I must go to do a little work. We can leave here at nine on Saturday and enjoy a hearty walk before stumbling upon the lovely house which could be yours before the year is out, God willing."

I stepped outside and inhaled the cool, uncomplicated air.

"Please wear suitable clothing, Alan, and a little knapsack if you have one."

"Ha, *I* am a proper walker." I looked him up and down. "I can't imagine you dressed in anything but shiny shoes and stylish clothes."

"I have an extensive outdoor wardrobe. Don't be late."

After our intense tête-à-tête I didn't feel up to going to Vicente's bar as planned, so I drove straight home, recalling the photos of that lovely house.

"I know that lovely house will never be ours, and I won't let Juanca be too intrusive, but it'll be fun to spend time with him in the great outdoors," I said to Inma that evening after I'd spilled the beans about our reconnaissance mission. In the end I'd reasoned that honesty was the best policy, partly because she wouldn't have believed there was no ulterior motive for our outing.

"Yes, I suppose it'll be different, but I thought you wished to find our new house without his help."

I sighed. "I did, and still do, but he knows everything about every house that's for sale. He's promised not to take a commission anyway."

"Ha!"

I explained why he wished to ingratiate himself with me.

"Hmm, yes, of course. Oh, well, the important thing is to find a place within our budget, because we've no idea how much you'll earn in your new job."

I stood up.

"Please don't start pacing around."

I sat down, but retained most of the air I'd inhaled to puff out my chest. "Well, the second half of January will be a sort of apprenticeship, but next month I hope to bring home two thousand, including my €500 fixed salary, although I might ask Fran to dispense with that and pay me a higher commission instead, because if I'm a success it'll be to my advantage and if I'm a flop, which I won't be, I don't want him to be out of pocket," I babbled.

She tittered. "When you deliver your sales patter to your customers, remember to breathe from time to time. As for the salary, you must take it."

"Why?"

"Because if you fail to sell much, it may be because the products aren't competitively priced or are simply not the best ones on the market. As you're going to spend three days a week trying your very hardest to sell them, you must have some recompense."

"All right, I'll take it for now. Oh, Juanca seems to think that I'll struggle to sell to Spaniards and ought to ask his advice before I attempt to."

She mused on this for a while. "Hmm, I'd start with some British people, if I were you, then maybe some other foreigners. Oh, by the way, we told Jorge he had to take some time off soon and he suggested the week beginning on the fourteenth."

"Ah, right… no! That's my first week. I can't possibly work at the bar too."

She pinched my cheek. "Don't worry, I asked him to choose a week in February and another in March."

"Phew, thank God for that. Oh, and what about the cook?"

"Alicia's already taken all her holidays up to April."

"Good. And Rosa?"

"Knowing her, she'll work the week she has left, so you'll just have Jorge's weeks."

"Right. Do you have any holidays left?"

"Er, I think after taking three months off I ought to work, don't you?"

"I guess so." I remembered something. "So you also doubt my ability to sell to Spaniards, do you?"

She shrugged. "You can try, but I think after a week in the bar you'll be better prepared to tackle them."

I tutted. "But I interact with lots of Spaniards, Inma." I tapped her right temple. "I already know what makes you tick." I rocked forward on the sofa but decided to remain seated. "My approach will be slightly different, of course, possibly stressing the financial savings to be made more than the environmental benefits, because you're a little backwards in that respect, generally speaking."

She chuckled. "Are we?"

"Yes, of the three electric cars I've spotted in town, two were driven by foreigners and one by a local businessman and town councillor, or so Juan told me."

"I'd like to have one."

"Really?"

"Yes, don't you feel that at least one of our cars ought to be electric?"

"Oh, yes, if not both. It'd make just the right impression on my customers."

"Yes, it would, so empty the cornflakes box and go to the bank, because we'll need over twenty thousand to buy the first one."

"Ah, yes, well, Rome... er, the new eco-friendly Rome won't be built in a day, will it? Let's get our dream home first, cover the roof with solar panels, then move on to... vehicular ecology after that."

"All right."

I switched on the TV and on seeing a Spanish soap opera I was about to change channels.

"No, leave it on, Alan."

"But we don't watch rubbish like this."

"Think of it as research for your new job."

By the time the adverts came on we'd witnessed a bitter argument, a cheesy scene with a sweet old lady and her granddaughter, a bit of extramarital sex, a spot of conniving between two men who were determined to destroy another's reputation, and a display of extreme envy over a neighbour's new (non-electric) car.

I muted the volume, as I can't abide adverts. "Wow, that was a bit hectic."

She chuckled. "Yes, in ten minutes you've witnessed Spaniards as you've rarely seen them, because I'm so sweet to you and shield you from unpleasant people."

"Ha ha… oh, I see, you're still thinking about me selling panels to them. Well, you're forgetting that I've been involved in the refurbishment and running of a hotel, interacting with many of your compatriots and never seeing anything like that, or not much. Not to mention all the hours I've spent in Vicente's bar, chewing the fat with those down to earth, no-nonsense men."

"We don't say to chew the fat in that context, Alan."

"I know, but you understand me."

"Oh, dear, you do have a selective memory."

"Have I?"

"Yes, think about Juan and Jesús's long-running feud, or Juanca and Cristóbal's falling out, or Arturo's problems with racism, or his attitude to Álvaro's sexual orientation, or that Gerardo fellow at the hotel."

I shivered. "The sneaky devil."

"Most Spaniards are pleasant and carefree on the surface, but some are prone to be devious, bitter and envious. In most of your dealings with folk you've either been in a position of authority, however tenuous, have possessed something they wanted, or have simply been treated well because you're an amusing foreigner." She smiled. "In the bar, on our side of the counter, you'll be at their service. The folk you already know will treat you much the same, but to others you'll be a mere minion to be ordered around. If they've had a bad morning they may take it out on you, as they'll imagine a middle-aged foreigner working as a waiter to be an inferior sort of being. Snobbery is another vice which we suffer from too, you see. To some folk status is everything."

"And what status will a solar panel salesman have in a Spaniard's eye?"

"Hmm, I'm not sure. Sales people are sometimes looked down on, but as you'll have a progressive sort of product they may respect you a little more, and... and... yes, of course!"

"What?"

She squeezed my hand. "You may not need much coaching from Juanca, as I think I've hit upon a possible key to your success."

"Really?"

"Yes, of all the deadly sins, I'm sure that envy is the one which Spaniards commit most often."

"Hmm, envidia, sí. But us British can be envious too."

"Yes, but I don't think you're in the same league as us. For instance, when Arvid and Randi got their solar panels, what did Cathy and Bernie think about them?"

"Er, I can't remember. I think they were more interested in their antics than their panels."

"And are you envious of Juanca's new BMW?"

"No, I don't like flashy cars."

"Or of Malcolm's wealth?"

"A bit, but I don't begrudge him it."

"Did Beth resent working for old Bill because he had plenty of money?"

"Not that I know of. What are you driving at? That Brits are angelically unenvious and Spaniards are eaten up by it?"

"Well..."

"I mean, you don't envy anyone, do you?"

"How do you know?"

"Well, you'd have told me... wouldn't you?"

She smiled. "All of us strive to hide our defects, Alan. When I saw Susana's lovely chalet in Asturias I felt a touch of envy, probably because we're both Murcians and come from a similar background."

"Oh, a touch of envy is normal, even healthy, as it makes us aspire to get on… a bit."

"And you'll remember that Natalia's father was a professional boxer."

I massaged the knuckles of my right hand and failed to make them crack, as usual. "Yes, but he never dared to face me."

"Just as well. Anyway, although he was Spanish champion for a while he never made all that much money, while a few of his colleagues, especially Javier Castillejo, who was the world champion at one time, had quite lavish lifestyles. Back then I felt genuine envy, because we seemed so close to success and riches, but I suppose I'm more mature now. Anyway, I feel sure that exploiting envy could be crucial when selling to Spaniards."

I nodded. "One-upmanship," I said in English, before explaining the expression.

"Yes, it happens a lot here."

"So how do I go about exploiting this tremendous envy?"

"I'm not sure." She closed her eyes. "Hmm, I'm visualising a… an episode which may be helpful."

"Tell me about it."

"Wait, it hasn't finished… hmm, yes… ha, a success." She opened her eyes and giggled. "How silly!"

She told me she'd pictured me entering Cathy and Bernie's compound, but the owners were a rather pijo (snobbish) Spanish couple. After they'd shut away their pair of vicious Dobermanns – an irrational fear of mine – they led me around to the porch and I began my sales patter, initially with little success, until I noticed the sun glinting on the panels on Arvid and Randi's house. I then pointed across the field and told them that my panels were more advanced and would also be positioned more correctly due to the orientation of their house. "So you end up walking away with an order for lots of panels."

I nodded. "Hmm, and maybe for a little wind turbine too, as presumably the folk in Randi and Arvid's house don't have one."

"Yes, I suppose this one-upmanship concept works in that way too, but I think pure envy is the simplest tool." Her smile faded and she began to chomp on her bottom lip.

"What now, dear?"

"I... I think you should push this idea to the back of your mind for now, Alan. In fact it might be better to forget about it altogether."

"But why? It's a great idea."

"Yes, but you know how, er... single-track your mind can become. Now I fear that you'll imagine all your potential Spanish customers to be consumed with envy."

I pictured a pair of green middle-class faces. "No, no, I'll know when to, er... turn on the envy tap."

"All right." She picked up the remote control. "More research?"

"No, let's watch a film."

She rifled through her box of DVDs. "How about this one of Othello with Orson Welles?"

"Er, isn't there a lot of envy in it?"

"More jealousy than envy."

"All right then."

3

After a relaxing couple of days during which I practised on my keyboard but sang very little, as it wasn't the same without good old Juanje, I felt a sense of glee on seeing Juanca's BMW pull up outside his office, as I meant to tire him out so much that by the time we reached the object of our expedition he'd be too knackered to pester them about selling their home. I climbed in and complimented him on his stylish walking clothes.

He stroked his green North Face fleece top. "Yes, I don't get out much." He patted his brown Berghaus trousers. "But when I do I like to be prepared."

I looked over at the empty rear seats. "But you may be a little underdressed. I know it's sunny, but it's only about ten degrees."

He chortled. "The rest of my gear's in the boot." He peered into my footwell. "Hmm, trainers."

"Walking trainers, perfect for today. Up north we bought all the waterproof gear, but I don't expect to get much use out of it until we return."

He lowered his window and sniffed. "One never knows. In the hills the weather can change just like that."

"Yes, Juanca."

We crawled along until the 30kph zone ended, then he put his foot down. In about six minutes we were quite close to Cathy and Bernie's house, so I took a look at the odometer. After whizzing east along a sinuous road for a while he pulled over on the outskirts of a tiny hamlet and pointed across the cultivated valley.

"You can see the house there, just below the pine trees. By following that ridge around the fields it's a three kilometres walk, but if you get tired we can stroll back along the road, only two kilometres."

I smiled. "Oh, I think I'll be all right."

"As you can see, the house isn't so far from Inma's bar."

"Er, no, not for you, but we don't all drive like maniacs." I checked the odometer. "You've covered the twenty-seven kilometres from near my sister's in… nineteen minutes, mostly on a minor road. That would take a prudent person at least half an hour, and the town's even further away, so that house isn't for us, I'm afraid."

"There are other towns, like Novelda and Aspe."

"But what about all my dear friends, including you?"

"Make new ones."

"Sorry, but today's going to be all about the walk, so zip up and let's be off."

We climbed out and he opened the boot. While he inspected the almost cloudless sky I stood gaping at all his stuff. As well as a large rucksack there were at least two coats, overtrousers, boots, poles and God knew what else. Rather than ridiculing the gear which would have equipped a modest alpine expedition, I kept shtum and waited for him to make his selection.

He put his hands on his hips and surveyed the scene, rather like Edmund Hillary on the morning of May 29th, 1953, I imagine.

"Hmm, I don't think I'll need my Mammut coat today."

I prodded it. "I think you could go to the North Pole in that."

He nodded. "You can, and to the South Pole too. No, I think my Fjällräven down jacket should be warm enough, and I can take my Helly Hansen waterproofs too, just in case. Now, which boots to wear? Hmm, my Garmonts are a little heavy and rather warm."

I bit my lip. "You could probably climb Himalayan peaks in them."

"You can. No, I think these lightweight Bestards will be adequate today."

"Yes, you can't beat a good pair of Bestards."

He looked at my feet. "What type are those?"

"The fifty euro type. Come on, let's get going."

Ten minutes later we set off and soon turned onto a rough track which gradually climbed towards the low ridge. Due to my lanky legs I was able to set a deceptively brisk pace without appearing to hurry, so Juanca was soon making full use of his state-of-the-art walking poles, thrusting them into the track with each stride.

"Do you really need those, Juanca?"

Crunch, crunch, crunch. "This way I employ more muscles and make it easier on the legs," he said, already panting slightly.

On reaching a flatter section I suggested he strap them to his rucksack. "They can't possibly be any use now."

Crunch, crunch, crunch. "Yes, they are. They help to stabilise the weight of my rucksack."

"Hmm, it does seem a bit heavy. What have you got in it?"

Crunch, crunch, crunch. "Just the bare essentials." He stopped and wiped his forehead with the back of his glove. "Ah, look at that view down towards the coast."

I looked at the dry and uninspiring terrain, as the little valley was the last verdant haven before the seemingly barren wastes began. "I guess the owners of that house really did choose the nearest green place to Elche, which isn't so far away."

"Yes. Listen."

"To what?"

"The silence, apart from a few chirping birds. We're a long way from civilisation here."

I glanced back at the hamlet. "Er, yes, quite a way."

"If anything happened to us up here, no-one would find us for ages."

"No, not for a while, but I don't anticipate any accidents."

"One never knows. One of us could stumble and break an ankle."

"Not in those boots, you couldn't."

"You then, but don't worry, I'm equipped for us to survive for at least forty-eight hours, if not longer. Come on, we've a long way to go."

After hiking along the ridge for a mile or so I suggested first scaling the summit above the pine woods, then descending through the trees to the house.

He stopped and adjusted his thermal hat.

"Take that damned thing off, Juanca, and those daft gloves too. They're only making you sweat. It's a lovely sunny day and not cold at all."

"You're forgetting the wind-chill factor."

I licked a finger and held it up. "What wind?"

"Yes, well, I didn't buy all this gear not to use it. The summit, eh?" He shielded his eyes and peered at the small hill about half a mile away. "Hmm, the approach appears to be feasible, but what about the woods below? There may not be a path down to the house."

"Oh, I'm sure we'll manage."

"All right, we'll attempt it, but let's take a break first."

He slung off his rucksack and while he was unfastening all the straps and toggles I pulled my little flask from my knapsack and unscrewed the top.

"What's that?"

"Coffee."

He frowned. "Put it away, please."

"Why?"

By way of reply he produced a dinky stove, a small gas canister, a tiny pan, a bottle of water, a set of high-tech camping cutlery and a few small rubbery containers.

"Good grief," I said in English.

He yanked out the tiniest folding stool I'd ever seen. "You can sit on this, as you're my guest. Now, you can have tea, coffee or one of my emergency energy drinks."

"Coffee, please."

"Would you like a dehydrated meal too, as used on a Spanish expedition to the Andean peaks last year?"

"Er, no thanks. I had a good breakfast not long ago."

"Hmm, me too. Oh, well, maybe later."

We were soon sipping sickly coffee with condensed milk. Juanca was enjoying every minute of our daring adventure, so I refrained from teasing him for the time being.

"What else have you got in that rucksack?" I said as I reached for it.

He slapped my hand. "You'll see as and when each item becomes necessary." He gazed up at the blue sky. "In a way it's a shame that meteorological conditions aren't a little more challenging, but for a first outing I guess we don't want too many surprises."

"So is this the first time you've used all this gear?"

"Yes."

"When did you buy it?"

"Oh, when my wife was… away, and I've been too busy since then. Right, let's pack up and press on to the summit." He surveyed the moderately steep slope from the summit to the house. "Will you get down there without poles?"

"I think I'll manage, although I suppose a rope would be handy."

His hand approached his rucksack, but he withdrew it. "Er, do you think all this a little excessive, Alan?"

I smiled. "No, it's like being ultra-modern boy scouts."

He rubbed his hands together. "Good. Pass me the stool."

From the not-so-towering summit the wooded north-westerly face sloping down to the house and the scrubby treeless expanse on the other side seemed like two different worlds. I pointed down at the house in its olive grove.

"I wonder how much longer the greenery will last in this valley."

"Long enough for Inma and you to enjoy it."

"Forget the house, Juanca. We aren't interested."

"Maybe not, but someone else will be."

"Come on, let's commence our descent."

"First I must extend my poles to compensate for the gradient."

Initially the trees were well spaced out, but before long the branches became entangled and the undergrowth more dense and prickly.

"This is typical of Spain," I moaned. "As hardly anyone walks there isn't even a footpath through lovely woods like these."

"Never fear," said Juanca with an ominous cackle, before opening his rucksack and sliding out a sheathed instrument.

"Oh, don't tell me you've brought a saw too?"

"No." He unsheathed it.

"I might have known."

So, armed with his machete – as used by a Spanish expedition to the Amazon rainforest, or so an able salesman had told him in the best outdoor shop in Madrid – he hacked his way through the undergrowth so effectively that I was soon asking to have a go.

He stopped and turned around. "Do you see now why I've come so fully equipped?"

"Well..."

"Do you?"

"Yes, Juanca."

"All right then, but first immortalise this moment on that crappy phone of yours."

"Be careful," I said as he slid the blade between his teeth with the sharp side facing away. I took a couple of snaps.

"Mmmm." He removed the blade. "How do I look?"

"Incongruous. Like a polar explorer near the equator. Look."

"Ha, very good." He proffered the machete. "Handle it with care, Alan, as it's extremely sharp."

"Wait." I whipped off my gilet, fleece and t-shirt. "I'm going for the jungle look." I wiped the blade before clamping my teeth around it.

"I'll use my phone, so I can post it on social media."

I tried to shake my head. "Mmmm!"

"There. Oh, how wild you look! I'll just... yes, that's it."

"Mmmm," I removed the blade. "What have you done?"

"Emailed it to Inma, of course. Right, get dressed and get to work."

I enjoyed thwacking a path through the dratted bushes with the machete and it wasn't long before we emerged onto a grassy track which led to the house.

"Here, you'd better put this away, as they'll probably find you unsubtle enough without a lethal weapon in your hand."

Back into the rucksack it went. "Leave the talking to me, Alan."

"As always."

In the event there was little talking to be done, as the lone Alsatian was surprisingly uncommunicative and there was nobody else at home. I strove to keep my delight to myself, but Juanca didn't seem too put out.

"I think it's a waiting game anyway. I'll call them soon and assess the state of play. If I feel they may be close to throwing in the towel, I'll buy an item or two of furniture. I assume they'll be down in Elche now, on such a lovely winter's day."

I peered through the metal fence. "The house looks even better than in the photos."

"Hmm, yes, I may have underestimated its value. More like 200,000, I think." He looked me up and down. "It's a shame that you're too cowardly to get a small mortgage, then you could aspire to places like this."

"Our aspirations are modest, but… hmm, I suppose if my sales go really well we could spend a bit more. They aren't in a great hurry to buy the cave house, you see, but they've hinted that they'd like to move in by the summer, which gives me several months to sell like a demon, and…"

"Please, Alan, no work talk. We're here to commune with nature." He lowered his rucksack to the ground. "Let's try those dehydrated meals now."

"I've brought sandwiches."

He frowned. "They're approaching their sell-by date."

"Oh, all right, but not here. Let's nip back into the woods."

While the water was boiling he allowed me to explore his cavernous rucksack, so I began to empty it.

"Waterproofs, a bivvy bag, a… what's this tinfoil thing?"

"An emergency sleeping bag."

"Hmm, maps, a compass, a whistle, a torch, a first aid kit."

"With a collapsible splint, in case you break your leg."

"Right. Ha, a rope, but a thin one."

"Easily capable of holding our entire weight."

"That's good to know. A… is this a flare?"

"Yes, the man fetched it from the aquatic department when I expressed concern about becoming stranded in the wilderness, and this too."

I flipped the cylindrical object from hand to hand.

"Be careful, Alan. It's a smoke grenade."

I laughed. "Oh, Juanca, they really saw you coming."

"What?"

"They've pulled your hair, selling you all this useless stuff. I'm surprised that a cunning salesman like you allowed it to happen."

He chuckled as he poured two bags of powdery stuff into the pan. "No, Alan, it was entirely my own fault. I went to Madrid for a change of scene, you see, and with a lot of cash after a recent sale. I entered the store with no clear intention, but soon embarked upon the spending frenzy whose results you can see before you."

"But why?"

He shrugged. "I enjoy buying nice things, and once I started I couldn't stop. I was a little down, you see, having realised that apart from money I didn't have all that much going for me, so I set about ridding myself of the wad of notes in my pocket." He prodded the rucksack with his foot. "I also bought a very expensive tent and sleeping bag, plus a few more things I can't recall right now." He stirred the gruel and tasted it. "I think this is ready."

"What the hell is it?" I said a few minutes later after rinsing a sticky mess from just about every surface of my buccal cavity.

He looked at the packet. "Er, it's supposed to be beef stew with barley. Maybe I didn't use enough water."

"Never mind. Have a sandwich."

"Gracias."

After sharing my coffee we headed back along the deserted road, and despite my offer he wouldn't hear of me carrying his rucksack.

"No, Alan. Who knows when I'll get the opportunity to use it again?"

"Any weekend you like. I'm always up for a walk, and I must say you're fitter than I expected you to be, lugging that tremendous weight around all morning."

"My work keeps me fit, always rushing here and there. When do you start selling the panels?"

"Oh, not for another week. I mean to take it easy until then."

He groaned. "Oh, Alan, with that attitude I doubt you'll ever have the wherewithal to buy the kind of house that Inma deserves."

"Eh? But what can I do without the latest catalogue and order forms?"

"Research, you chump. As these solar appliances are so highly visible you can tour your whole sales area, noting down every possible customer. As you won't be making any calls, in a week you'll be able to drive along every road, lane and track, devising a route which will serve you well for months or even years to come. That's what I'd do anyway. What's wrong?"

This revelation had caused the blood to rush from my legs to my brain and I'd staggered to a halt. "I'm only working three days a week," I muttered.

"Humph! You're only *paid* to work three days a week. Look back at the house." I obeyed. "Because unless you change your attitude, you're never going to possess anything remotely like it. Now, get walking and listen to me…"

"Hola, Tarzán," Inma said a couple of hours later. "What a funny photo he sent me… oh, what's the matter?"

I groaned as I fell into her arms. "Juanca's been bullying me," I whimpered.

"With that big knife?"

"No, with his harsh words about my attitude to work. True words too, I'm afraid, because instead of relishing the prospect of following his wise advice, I... I... oh, I don't know."

She stroked my hair. "There, there. Come and sit down and tell me all about it."

She soon cheered me up by advising me to use satellite maps to study the lay of the land. "There's little point in driving around all week long and it would only make you fret about the forthcoming challenge."

"Yes, yes, I can plan it all on the computer. Good thinking, love."

"Now tell me about your walk."

I summarised the expedition in an amusing way, before concluding that Juanca and I had grown closer after our shared experience. "Especially after he confessed to being a, er... comprahólico."

"A what?"

"We say shopaholic."

"A compulsive shopper, yes." She sighed. "How sad. I hope he'll serve as a warning to you."

"Er, why?"

"Because his lifelong obsession with money has made him unable to enjoy the simple things in life, like walking, in a normal way." She squeezed my hand. "I hope you becoming a salesman won't corrupt your soul as it has his."

I reflected on the leisurely week ahead which I'd snatched from the jaws of labour. "There's not much danger of that, dear." My relieved smile turned into a frown.

"Oh, what now?"

"That house was lovely, you know, and maybe Juanca's right and we'll never be able to afford anything like it."

"Oh, what rubbish! We could easily get a mortgage and buy a four-bedroom house with a pool, but that would mean committing ourselves to working for the next fifteen or twenty years."

I gulped, as I never like hearing the W-word and a considerable length of time uttered in the same breath. "I'll be fifty-two in March," I murmured.

"Exactly." She smiled. "Who knows, when you're out and about chatting to people you may find that rather than wishing to buy solar panels they want to sell their house, or they know a neighbour who wants to sell theirs."

"Hmm, yes, yes... YES!"

"Ouch!" She rubbed her ear.

"Sorry, dear, but you've just said the truest thing since... since the last true thing you said. Yes, yes, I can picture myself walking into a pretty old house on the edge of a hamlet, with no Dobermanns, and finding a pleasant, elderly couple who scoff at the idea of sticking panels on their roof because their greatest desire is to move to town to be near their grandchildren. Then, over the coffee they've kindly served me, I'll subtly mention that my charming wife and I would love to live in a quiet place like theirs, and little by little the subject of a possible sale will arise. 'But we want to keep the house for the summers,' he'll say. 'Are we sure about that?' says she. 'Think of the lovely town house we could buy, instead of that third-floor flat we've been considering.' 'Hmm, you have a point, dear. So, young man, are you–'"

"Alan."

"'Serious about buying our...' What?"

"You sound like Zefe. Don't get your hopes up too much."

"But something like that could happen, couldn't it?"

"Possibly. Just keep your eyes and ears open."

I frowned. "Hmm, and that explains why Juanca said he wished to follow my progress closely, in order to advise me. Ha, he just wants me to tip him off about possible sellers, the rogue."

"Well, he can hardly fail to see that you'll be in the perfect position to hear all the house-related gossip, but no doubt he'll make it worth your while."

"Yes... oh, that old chestnut again."

"Castaña?"

"I mean the same old story. Before I know it I'll be sucked into another fat envelope."

She tittered. "You are expressing yourself strangely today. When are you meeting your boss?"

"Next Friday."

"Then don't give it another thought until then. Don't even look at the map. Enjoy your last few days of freedom by seeing your friends and trying to relax."

I smiled. "Yes, I will."

4

Easier said than done, of course, especially while playing golf with Malcolm near Villena on a chilly Tuesday morning. Until the fifth hole he espoused the same viewpoint as Juanca, contending that three-day weeks were for wimps and that I ought to get my bloody finger out and sweet-talk every man, woman and child into buying solar panels.

I fluffed my putt, then tapped in the ball. "Ha, children too, eh?"

"Yes, though not directly. You should approach the education authority and tell them all their schools ought to go green."

"Er, I think that's a bit ambitious, Malcolm."

"I'd do it like a shot." He sank a six-footer. "That's four-one. Hmm, what advice can I give to a slacker like you?" I handed him his ball and shouldered his golf bag, into which he thrust his putter. "You've always got to think outside the box, you see, and... hmm, box, blocks... yes, you'll be visiting blocks of flats, I take it?"

"Of course not. They can hardly fill their balconies with panels, even if they are correctly orientated. The orientation is crucial, you see. I've been reading up on it and–"

"On the roof, you wally. The big flat roof, pointing at the sky. These blocks of flats have a sort of community, don't they?"

"Do they?"

"Yes, to maintain the lifts and whatnot. So, you find the community boss man and propose a great big square of panels, like a gigantic waffle, sucking in the sun's rays and saving them a fortune."

"Ha, I bet I'd have to waffle a lot to get them to do that," I said, tickled by my pun.

He gazed at me grimly. "Don't you have an ounce of ambition in you, Alan?"

"Er, yes, at least an ounce, if not more."

On the way to the sixth he explained what was in store for me if I didn't step out of my little comfort zone and into his rather large one. I'd spend my days trailing from chalet to chalet, and as I wouldn't even have the balls to stick my foot in the door I'd be rebuffed time and time again. "Then, finally, some sucker lets you in and by some miracle you make a sale."

"That's a relief."

"How much does a decent set of panels with all the gubbins to make them work cost?"

As I'd done my homework I was able to tell him that a six-panel kit with a 5000W, 48V inverter and three lithium batteries, plus a platform, cables, connectors and whatnot could be had for about €7000. "That's big enough to power a house, as long as it's mostly sunny and they use LED lights and... well, don't use much energy."

"Sounds a bit crap to me."

"Yes, well, my boss reckons that's the kit that'll sell most and if it does he'll be able to get a discount, so we'll both be pushing that one."

"And how much is your commission?"

"Six percent," I mumbled.

"What?"

"Six percent, unless I forego my five hundred a month and… and ask for more."

He whipped out a hefty club. "Do you know what I'd tell the pillock?"

"Er, go on."

"Tee up my ball."

"What?"

"Tee up my ball."

I obeyed.

"I'd tell him to give me ten percent and to hell with that joke of a salary. Do you know how many of my salesmen get a salary?"

"Er, none?"

"Co-rrect. A salesman's there to sell, and if he can't sell he's neither use nor ornament; no good to me or to himself, or herself. So, you tell that joker to give you ten percent and keep his alms. Is he new to this game too?"

"Yes, I believe so."

"I might have known. He sounds as soft as you."

"He's a very nice man."

"That's what I mean. I didn't get where I am today by being nice to people."

I sniggered. "No, CJ."

"Eh?"

"CJ, Reggie Perrin's boss."

"Who?"

I explained.

"Ha, I didn't have time to watch TV back in the seventies, or any other decade for that matter. I didn't get where... so, let's see, ten percent of seven grand is seven hundred." He gripped his club and smirked at me. "How many sales do you hope to make in a week?"

"Well, one a week would provide me with a really good salary."

"Bah!" He whacked the ball. "Shite."

"Good shot, on the seventh. You don't know your own strength."

As luck would have it, my shot with the three-iron fell pitifully short.

He sniggered deeply from the diaphragm. "That says it all, Alan. Aim low and achieve sod all."

"Yes, and aim high and... and end up God knows where. I'm going to win this hole to teach you a lesson in moderation."

"Ha!" He tossed me the club, grabbed an iron, and stomped off, slightly fleeter of foot after getting down to sixteen stone as he'd assured me he would back in September.

I did in fact win the hole by one shot, but that didn't stop him from returning to the subject of flats.

"Every Spanish town's full of them and I reckon just one sale could net you five grand, if not more. Instead of farting about in the country, you should be going from block to block, finding the community boss and putting it to him. If he's not up for it, rally the neighbours. Knock on every door in the place and get them on your side. Blind them with science, mesmerise them with figures, show them what they'll save, sew up the deal, then onto the next block, day after day, week after week. Your turn."

I shuffled over and had to crouch to stick in my tee, so weak had my knees become.

"Mention it to your boss. He'll like the idea."

"Yes, Malcolm." I resolved not to mention it to Fran in case he liked the idea. As you can imagine, his proposal was anathema to a man like me. Although more than happy to potter around the countryside in the hope of making a sale now and then, an aggressive urban campaign wasn't my cup of tea at all. When Malcolm abruptly changed the subject I was ever so grateful, so despite not wishing to become involved I made all the right noises, simply to put an end to the solar grilling that threatened to cause me many a sleepless night.

"Oh, Angela's finally decided to sell the hotel," was the fateful statement.

"Oh, right. Is she sad about it?"

"Not really. She's already looking at places to buy back in Norfolk, so I guess we'll be going home soon."

"Do you have a nice house there?"

He slid out his iPhone and showed me a photo.

"Right, yes, it looks a bit like Versailles."

"It's supposed to, though it's a lot smaller, of course."

"Hmm, yes, only twelve windows."

"It's still too big, but what can you do if you're a multi-millionaire? People expect it of you. Personally I couldn't care less about most of the things that money can buy. I've just enjoyed making it. Anyway, it's time to get your skates on and find me a buyer."

So it was that I turned an incipient shake of the head into a buoyant bout of nodding. "Of course."

He eyed me suspiciously. "Tee off."

I struck the ball well and it reached the edge of the green. "Not too hard, Malcolm."

"I'll try." His ever so gentle drive placed his ball within a couple of yards of mine. "Hmm, looks like we're in sync for once."

"Yes." Bag on shoulder, I turned around to receive his club. On completing my twirl I beheld a mischievous grin.

"So, how do you plan to go about selling it?"

"Well, I... I..."

"It's all right. I won't put you on the spot."

"Thanks."

"You've got the rest of the hole to convince me not to give the job to someone else. Come on."

My putting had never been worse, but it bought me enough time to come up with an idea which I hoped would meet with his approval, though I feared it might smack of my usual lack of initiative and fondness for delegation.

"Five-two. Well?"

"Well..."

He raised his putter. "And if I hear the word wanker I'll clobber you."

"Juanc... he didn't even cross my mind," I lied, as his fawning countenance had popped straight into it, then made a speedy exit when I remembered that Malcolm couldn't abide the man. "No, I suggest – and this may seem unadventurous, but I'll tell you anyway – that we find an estate agency which specialises in hotel sales on a national or even international scale." I held my breath.

"Go on."

"I'm sure that a serious setup like that will take a fixed commission which oughtn't to be very high, so once you know how much it is, you'll be able to set your price."

"Hmm." He slid his putter into the bag. "You're thinking even bigger than me, for once."

I believe I coloured slightly.

"I was thinking that some rich Valencian bloke might want to give the hotel a go, or turn it into a private home, but I'm liking your idea more and more. Hmm, yes, let's get it on the worldwide market. Ha, who knows, some Arab oil sheik or Russian mafioso might snap it up."

"Exactly." I led the way to the next hole. "In that case it might not matter that the hotel isn't doing well."

"Doing well? It's bloody empty. There's only your mate Arturo and two more still working, but not for long." He sighed. "Any hotelier with half a brain would run a mile, and anyone who wants to turn it back into a house won't pay enough. I'm determined to recoup my money, you see. I've never lost money on property and I don't mean to start now."

I then recalled something which soon led to my greatest idea since asking Inma to step out with me. "Malcolm, do you remember the early days of the hotel?"

He grunted noncommittally.

"How you, er... enticed some of your workers to come out for a free holiday."

"Hmm."

"Well, you could do the same thing again, but on a grander scale. Yes, once we've generated some interest we'll have to stipulate a certain week for viewing, then make sure the place is buzzing when they arrive."

"I'm not made of money, Alan."

"Well... ha, yes, that's it. We don't need your employees. We can get local people to come for a free break."

"What about the staff to look after them?"

I grinned. "Locals too. I know folk who'll be up for it." I pictured Bernie dressed as a waiter, Cathy as a cook, Juan posing as a chauffeur, Jesús digging a flower bed, Álvaro doing the accounts, Inma on reception, and me as the manager.

"Alan?"

"And Diego behind the bar, ha ha... oh, what?"

"It's a bloody preposterous idea."

I sighed and my troupe evaporated. "Yes, I suppose it is."

"But I like it. I like it a lot." He cackled. "In fact it's right up my street."

"I'm glad you approve." A minor impediment then occurred to me. "Oh, but what about when they ask to see the books?"

He swiped the air. "Oh, bugger the books. First impressions are what count in this game. There'll be time enough to come up with an excuse for six lousy months once they're gagging to get their hands on the place." His hand came down on my shoulder with great force. "I take back any bad things I've said about you. You're a genius."

I tried and failed to shrug. "Oh…"

"And you're going to arrange it all, right down to the last detail."

Gulp. "Yes, Malcolm."

"Let's play."

Back in the clubhouse after my seven-two defeat he was so pleased with me that he decided not to drag me around another nine holes as he usually did. As I sipped a real beer I didn't feel quite as sanguine as he looked, because it was one thing to pass the buck to a top-notch estate agency and quite another to populate the hotel on a given week which probably wouldn't be chosen until the last minute. What had seemed like a jolly jape when I'd thought of it now threatened to cause me far more sleepless nights than touting panels around a few blocks of flat.

"You seem to be thinking deeply, Alan."

Wallowing in imminent misery, I thought. "Yes, pondering on the logistics of my idea."

"Really?"

"Yes."

He grinned. "And not about how much you stand to make?"

"Eh? That hadn't even crossed my mind."

He shook his massive head. "You know, I actually believe you."

"It's true."

"Oh dear, oh dear. What are we going to do with you?"

Assuming it to be a rhetorical question, I sipped and shrugged.

"Look, Alan, I mean to leave Spain with €750,000 in my pocket, or in the bank. Either way suits me. Whatever you make on top of that, after this agency and all your pals have been paid, is down to you."

"Oh, I've given up taking commissions for doing nothing. I want to go out to work and earn my money honestly for once."

"Yeah, by getting commissions on solar panels. Anyway, you won't be doing nothing this time. As you don't like the C-word, though God knows why, just think of it as a job of work. Decide how much you want to pay yourself, then add that to the 750 grand too."

"I…"

"But don't sell yourself short. I'm aware that this will eat into your panel selling time, so factor in all the commissions you might have got."

"Hmm, according to you, not many."

"Or a lot, given your uncanny brilliance at times. I'm not a greedy man, Alan."

"No."

"And of all the folk I've met in Spain you're just about the only one I've got any time for."

"Ta."

"I'd like to see you better yourself."

"Ah."

"And I don't mind giving you a leg up, if you've got the gumption to take it."

"Hmm."

"I mean, what's twenty or thirty grand to me? I'll tell you. A drop in the ocean, a season in the Caribbean, half a car that I'll hardly ever drive, a fraction of Angela's next little project. In short, neither here nor there."

"I see."

"Grasp it, Alan."

"Yes. Er, what?"

"Twenty or thirty grand."

"Ha, don't be daft."

He groaned. "Look, you dozy sod, that hotel, when they see it buzzing, as you put it, will be worth way more than seven-fifty, as you'll see when you find this agency. That's chickenfeed for a business that could turn over two or three hundred thousand a year, on top of what that fine building is actually worth."

"But… making it buzz will be a bit deceptive, won't it?"

"Bah, who cares? Who do you think's gonna buy it, a retired vicar and his wife? No, some great big heartless chain will take it on." He raised a forefinger. "Or, even better, some criminal capo who'll make it his rural retreat, with a helipad in case the cops move in, ha ha."

I imagined Spain being flooded with heroin from a place which I'd sold. "Oh, all this is getting a bit much for me, Malcolm. Maybe you should speak to Juanca instead."

"No wanker!" he boomed, causing a couple of foreign guys to glance over then quickly look away. He stood up and tossed a €20 note onto the table. "Come on."

Fearing that another round and more haranguing were in store for me, I trudged out behind him, wishing I'd never had that damned stupid idea. Although his mention of twenty or thirty grand had made me picture the house in the olive grove, it all seemed like an immense headache peppered with multiple pitfalls.

On realising, I believe, that I'd been shoved about a thousand miles outside my comfort zone, in the car park he tried to reassure me.

"Look, find the best agency and get them to call me, in English. Leave that side of things to me and just start recruiting folk for our busy week."

"All right, but what if the agency says that a… a fixed viewing week is no good?"

"Leave that to me."

"And what if they ask to see the books right away?"

"Leave that to me."

"And what if–"

"Whatever it is, leave it to me. I know how to deal with these people."

"Yes, Malcolm."

"And you'll know how to find waiters and cooks and chambermaids and receptionists, plus a couple of dozen guests."

"Ye… yes, Malcolm."

He grasped his golf bag for the first time that day and made for his Land Cruiser. "Think of it as a challenge, and a bit of a lark," he said over his shoulder.

"Yes, Malcolm," I mouthed, but the words failed to emerge.

Not wishing to make a habit of it, on arriving home I refrained from falling into Inma's arms, instead opting to collapse onto the sofa and curl into a foetal position.

"Oh, dear, what's happened now?"

I pushed myself up and asked her to sit down, before telling her my woeful tale. "So you see, just to stop him harping on about blocks of flats I've got myself into a real mess."

Her tinkly laughter rang out. "Oh, just imagine all those people filling the hotel! It'll be such good fun. I'd like to be a chambermaid, just wandering around with sheets and watching everybody in action."

I sighed. "I don't think you understand the magnitude of this undertaking, Inma. We're talking about filling the rooms with folk for five days and catering to their every whim. It's a logistical nightmare which will make my life a misery until it's over."

"Don't be silly. No-one needs to sleep there at all."

"Eh?"

"Look, we get our helpers lined up, then when potential buyers come to visit we spring into action. Rosa and I will close the bar and we'll all come to help. Hotels aren't normally so busy during the day, so we'll have maybe a fifteen guests toing and froing before a dozen of them sit down to lunch. When the buyer leaves in the afternoon they can all go home with a token of Malcolm's appreciation in their pockets."

"What if they wish to spend the night?"

"Then we'll adapt."

"What if several buyers want to come?"

"Then we'll do it several times. The idea of stipulating a particular week wouldn't work anyway."

"No, I guess not." I finally stopped frowning and took her hand. "Inma, I like the fact that you've said 'we' several times. It suggests that you really mean to share this burden with me."

"Of course I do."

I kissed her cheek. "You're so sweet."

"I can't let you imperil so much money, can I? That twenty or thirty thousand euros will come in *very* handy."

"Ah, I see. So it's pure avarice that's motivating you."

"Of course, and a desire to stop you having a nervous breakdown. This solar panel selling scheme will be quite enough for me to put up with, so find a good agency for Malcolm and try to forget about the whole thing for the time being."

I laid my throbbing head on her shoulder. "It won't be easy."

"Try. Anyway, I doubt anything will come of it. Fun things like this have a habit of not happening. Don't even mention it to anyone yet. We don't want too many people to know about it, and news spreads like wildfire from Vicente's bar, and ours too."

"Hmm, true. Ah, I feel better already." I flexed my fingers. "I do believe I'll play my keyboard a little before lunch."

"Find an agency first, then you can play all afternoon while I'm at work."

"All right. Hmm, you haven't done much drawing since we got back, and you've scarcely touched your paints."

She shrugged. "I know. It isn't the same here. There's no sea to paint and... well, we won't go into that now."

"Go into what?"

"Oh, nothing. Get to work."

"Sí, cariño."

Within the hour I'd located three suitable estate agencies online and called two of them. They were both more than happy to have an English-speaking member of staff call Malcolm, so I sent him an email, switched off the laptop, and resolved to push the whole affair into the cobwebbed recesses of my mind. Over lunch I asked Inma if she thought I should try to sell panels to the odd block of flats in town.

"Of course not. Every community will have been bombarded with offers to install them and you couldn't compete with those companies anyway. Forget about that silly idea."

"Oh, Inma, how you soothe my troubled mind, time and time again!"

"Yes. Dig up some onions later."

"Of course. Nothing would give me greater pleasure."

While extracting those vitamin-packed bulbs in the fading light I reflected that Bernie had the right idea. Communing with nature, even from the end of a spade, was a damn sight better than getting involved in irksome money-making schemes. I gazed over at our dead almond trees, but alas, it was too late to do anything about them now. After ten whole minutes of honest toil I'd filled my little bucket and was about to embark on a spot of weeding when I saw Zefe and Álvaro creeping up the track. After achieving a measure of serenity, the last thing I wanted was to hear the old goat's nonsense just then, so I busied myself with the hoe and hoped he wasn't in a tiresome mood.

Happily he appeared to be in a placid state of mind, until I remembered one of my resolutions and suggested to Álvaro that we take a walk the following day.

"Yes, I'd like that, Alan."

"We could walk over to the next hamlet, then return along a rough path which goes over the hill and comes out just along there, by the end of the field. It's about four kilometres and quite steep in places, but it's the best circular walk from here."

"That's all right. I need the exercise."

"Too far for me," said Zefe.

"Er, you're not coming," I said.

He raised a stick a few inches, then stabbed it into the earth. "And what am I supposed to do then?"

"We'll only be away for a couple of hours," I said, as I intended to take a flask and chill out for a while up in the sparse pine wood.

"We'll go shopping in the afternoon," Álvaro said to him, then turned to me. "He always enjoys pushing the trolley and pestering the housewives."

Zefe growled and insisted that he wanted to come walking with us. He looked up the hill. "I can get up there all right, given time."

I stabbed the hoe into the earth. "Don't be so selfish. Álvaro can't be at your beck and call all day long. Think about him for once."

"If I can walk up here, I can walk up there," he whined.

Álvaro then slowly raised his arm and pointed in the direction of his house. "Go home, Zefe. I'm sick of the sight of you."

I silenced my gasp with my hand, then steeled myself for the old man's reaction to this gross impertinence. Álvaro was within range of his right-hand stick, but didn't move a muscle. I stepped into Zefe's line of vision, rather like a torero trying to catch the bull's eye, but instead of swiping out or uttering a string of curses his eyes didn't leave the ground as he turned around and began to plod down the track. After gaping at the receding figure for a while I turned to see Álvaro calmly weeding the potatoes. On recovering the power of speech I elected to remain silent for a while longer and observe the spectacle of this suddenly strong and silent man, hoeing away contentedly, or so it seemed. On completing the row he lay down the hoe and approached me.

"Zeferino may be going back to live in his flat, Alan."

"Really?"

He nodded. "During the last couple of days he's become unbearable. Do you remember our conversation on New Year's Day?"

"Vividly."

"Well, on returning home he went on chattering about his inheritance and the gold which he assured me he'd sold in Caracas. I put it down to high spirits and humoured him, as usual, but the following morning he continued in the same vein. He felt especially delighted to have beguiled your brother-in-law with his tale, and you too to a lesser extent. In his warped mind he felt he had us all under a spell and didn't cease to accuse me of having mercenary motives, until this afternoon."

"What happened?"

"He called me a bespectacled, bearded vulture, circling its prey, so I told him that our period of cohabitation had gone on for long enough." He smirked and shook his head. "I spoke without thinking, but on reflection I didn't regret my words, especially after witnessing the effect they had upon him."

"Shock?"

"Precisely. Shocked silence, then mumbled apologies, then a solemn promise to behave better." He slapped the dust from his hands. "But you've just seen how long that promise has lasted. Could you give me a glass of wine?"

"Of course, come on."

Back at the house I lit the stove and we settled down at the dining table to plan the remainder of Zefe's days. I suggested readying his flat for his return, but using it as a punishment cell rather than a permanent abode.

"When he misbehaves you can drive him to town and dump him there for a day or two. That should help to keep him on the straight and narrow."

"Pardon?"

"That should make him behave."

"Hmm, I hope the threat of it will be enough, as I'd hate to think of anything happening to him alone there." He sighed. "What I really need is someone else to share the burden."

I sipped my wine, but the glass wasn't big enough to hide behind. "Yes, well…"

"Oh, I don't mean you. We need someone different, someone new, someone strict who won't be sucked into his mind games." He chuckled. "I can sort of picture a rather brusque and humourless woman who'll boss him around and make him realise how lucky he is to live with someone as compliant as me. I've considered looking for some kind of carer, but I can't really afford it and of course he'd never agree to pay for a person who'd be there expressly to keep him in order. I believe that even the threat of such a forceful female would be enough to scare the life out of him, but I know so few people."

"Hmm, my sister would be perfect, had she not met him already. She wouldn't agree anyway, as she's got her own oldies to see in town. I wonder if Rosa... but, no, she's far too busy. You know, I don't know many women either."

"Oh, well, let's hope the threat of the flat does the trick."

"Although I suppose, hmm... ooh, and then there's... yes, she'd be even better." I cackled fiendishly. "Oh, yes! Álvaro, I may have a double-pronged plan of attack, although I imagine each prong would arrive separately, ha ha."

He glanced at the half-empty bottle.

"No, I'm not drunk, although it may have gone to my head a little," I said, before telling him about the two people I had in mind. "In each case we'd have to hope for an effective initial visit, but of course he won't know where they've appeared from. What do you think?"

"Oh, I don't know, Alan. It seems like a plan designed more to amuse you... us than a serious aid to making him behave."

"Well I believe it might work, and what if we do have a laugh at his expense? It's about time he got a taste of his own medicine."

"All right. I'd better get back now."

"And I'll consult Inma about it, as always."

After agreeing to meet for our walk at ten the next morning I saw him out.

"It sounds to me like you just want to have a bit of fun at the old rascal's expense," Inma said shortly after her return from work. "But at least this silly idea has taken your mind off your own worries, for which I'm grateful."

I agreed that my recently hatched plot had proved to be a good antidote to my hotel-related anxieties. "So what do you think?"

"Not Beth. We don't know her nearly well enough to ask such a favour of her."

"No, I guess not. She just sprang to mind as the right type, but she's probably miffed that instead of making five thousand from Liz and Ben she'll get nothing. So that just leaves my other prong."

"What?"

"My other option. Will Natalia be up for it, do you think?"

"Hmm, she's promised to visit soon, but she always says that. Do you know, apart from that day at my parents' at Christmas I haven't seen her since the summer."

"Did she tell you why she didn't come to see us in Asturias?"

"Oh, busy with her studies, she said, and her latest boyfriend, I suspect." She moved her head from side to side and her lips began to twitch. "Hmm, maybe if we give her a mission to accomplish she'll be more inclined to make the trip."

"Yes, just tell her she has to tame an especially headstrong old man."

"No, that won't do. Somehow or other we'll have to give it a... an anthropological twist. Something that'll give her a sense of her own importance. Yes, as she's such a conceited little señorita these days I think that might convince her to come."

I then slapped my forehead, as people do in books, but which I really do when I feel I've been especially stupid. "Oh, damn it! But they've met before, the time she came alone when Zefe was in the annex, and again at our wedding party."

"I don't believe she even saw him here, and at the party I doubt they spoke. It won't matter anyway." She yawned. "Let me sleep on it. I'm sure to think of something by tomorrow."

"Ah, once again you come to the rescue."

"To rescue a foolish idea which I mean to turn to my advantage. Oh, I know it's inevitable that she and I will grow apart, but I would like to see her more often."

I planted a kiss on her ruffled brow. "Then this is your chance. Fire her up and she'll be here like a shot."

"I hope so." She glanced at my old solar panel catalogue on the coffee table and chuckled.

"What?"

"Oh, nothing." She tapped her head. "Just something else to add to my nocturnal thought processes."

So it was that the following cold and hazy morning I was able to tell Álvaro that our fairy god-daughter was likely to arrive sometime soon and get to work on his bothersome boarder.

"Hmm, Natalia, yes, a spirited young lady, I believe, but what will she do?"

"I don't know yet, but rest assured that whatever it is, Zefe will never be the same again."

"Er, I'm not sure I like the sound of that, Alan."

"Don't worry, you can put your trust in Inma's judgement. I always do. Drink up and we'll head down the hill."

5

At about half past one on Monday afternoon I was walking, or rather driving, on air. I'd visited only three British-owned chalets – identified by the large expanses of gravel and hideous ornaments – and after two polite rebuffs had just made a sale, or as near as dammit, because the sixty-something couple from Chippenham had promised to call me when they'd made up their minds between the economical 3000W kit and the downright cheap 2000W one. Neither would net me a fortune, it was true, and wouldn't provide enough power to make toast and boil a kettle at the same time, but that's what the charming pair wanted to begin with and I knew better than to pressure them excessively. Oh, they'd been like putty in my hands and the beauty of it was that I wouldn't have to do another thing! The company we were selling for would perform the installation and inform them about possible grants, so all I had to do was sit back and wait for my six percent.

Only six percent, because on Friday Fran had advised me against becoming a commission-only sales agent, which would entail being self-employed and having to make the 'autónomos' payments of about €300 a month, not to mention all the tiresome tax paperwork, a headache which Inma and Rosa suffered every spring. So, I calculated as I headed for Vicente's bar, after only three hours' work I'd already made at least €200 to add to my modest salary. By the time I parked the car I'd estimated that my initial half-month's earning should easily top the two thousand mark, because by then I too believed that three-day weeks were for unambitious wimps. So, when I really got the hang of it I ought to be looking at a cool five grand a month, even more than the amount which Fran had mentioned during our first meeting back in November.

As I swaggered along the street it struck me that Fran might have had his own interests at heart when persuading me to be a mere employee, because due to the projected volume of my sales he basically had a walking goldmine on his books. Ha, well, when I'd sold a few hundred thousand watts' worth of panels we'd see about that. If he didn't raise my commission I'd simply have a word with the company and tell them to look at my area on the live version of Google Earth. On seeing a veritable constellation of rooftop plaques glinting in the sunlight they'd probably cut poor old Fran out of the equation and give me the whole province to get my teeth into. I sniggering softly as I opened the door and warned myself not to let my success go to my head.

"A beer for me," I said to Vicente. "And whatever these chaps are having."

"Juan and Jesús?"

"All of them."

"Is it your birthday or something?"

I chuckled gutturally. "In a manner of speaking."

"Is something the matter with your neck?"

"No. Why?"

"Oh, by the way your chin's sticking in the air I thought you might have pulled a muscle or something."

I made a ten-degree adjustment before joining my pals.

Juan looked me up and down. "Have you won the lottery or something?"

I chuckled gutturally again, something I might have picked up from Malcolm. "In a manner of speaking."

When a couple of men raised their glasses and muttered their thanks, Jesús ordered wine and a tapa of squid, before eyeing me wryly. "He must have had some good news. Have you sold an expensive coin or something?"

"Oh, I no longer have time for my little hobbies. How are things on your land?"

"All right. There's a lot of ploughing to do at this time of year, but fortunately I'm still fit enough to do it."

Juan looked away, no doubt fearing that the subject of his so-far successful battle with prostate cancer was about to rear its repetitive head. I didn't flinch, however, as in my sanguine state I felt in the mood for a challenge.

"Bernie's been ploughing a lot too, but he complains of the chilly mornings we've been having."

Jesús shrugged. "One gets used to them."

"Yes, but he says he needs a cosy little refuge like yours, where he can warm himself up," I lied.

He eyed me over the rim of his glass. "Hmm, I see. Vicente! Another wine."

"Do you use the electric heater a lot?" I asked, as although he had a small wood-burning stove he could seldom be bothered to light it.

"A little."

"Expensive things to run. You really need a couple of solar panels, or maybe more."

"What for?"

I grinned before playing the first of my two trump cards. "To make money, of course."

"To *make* money?"

"Claro. It's a little-known fact that by selling excess energy back to the electricity network many owners of solar panels make considerable sums. As your consumption will be negligible most of the time, you'll be earning money day after day, week after week, month after–"

"Whoa! But the panels have to be paid for."

"Bah, two or three thousand, which you'll soon recoup," I said, although I suspected it might take a number of years.

"Hmm, I see."

I believe he was picturing the sun's rays making a beeline for his bank account, but to prise so much money out of such a penny-pincher would be no easy task, so I decided to play the card which Inma had added to my deck.

"And just think, you'll be the envy of all the other farmers."

"No, they'll just think he's finally lost his mind," said Juan.

I smiled. "Maybe, but not for long. They might scoff at the ultramodern addition to his casita, but they'll soon be asking themselves, 'If a wise and cautious man like Jesús has installed those things, he must have done so for a good reason.'" I looked around the bar, still busy as lunchtime approached. "It'll soon become a talking point here and Jesús may find himself becoming the centre of attention."

"Oh, I wouldn't like that," said he, but the increased ruddiness of his cheeks told me I might have stumbled upon yet another trump card.

I felt like whipping the folded leaflet from my rear pocket, but my instinct told me to bide my time. Instead I launched into a short lecture on how solar power was being woefully underexploited in southern Spain. "…and just think of all those abandoned fields. A person of initiative could become an important energy supplier merely by investing in a hectare or two of panels."

"I've seen several fields of panels, some of them large, rotating ones," said Juan.

"Yes, a few astute, forward-thinking farmers are already harnessing the sun's rays on their surplus land." I chuckled and shook my head. "It must be just about the easiest way to make money ever invented. I mean, one doesn't need to do anything at all, just install them and sit back to watch one's bank balance grow." I thought the spittle which had gathered between Jesús's lips a promising sign, so I turned my attention to Juan, an even tougher nut to crack.

"And those of us who don't possess land oughtn't to miss out either. I'm already making enquiries about some of the long-abandoned fields near Bernie's house, but I shan't tell them what I want it for, oh no, or the price will suddenly go up, ha ha!" I sighed. "It's a shame we're selling the cave house, or I'd have those dead trees out in a jiffy and that eyesore of a field would soon be the glittering jewel of the valley. You ought to think about buying a field while they're cheap, Juan, before word gets out and folk are fighting over them."

He gazed at me dolefully, before raising his hand and grasping his thumb. "One, no land around here is really cheap. Two, the cost of the panels would be astronomical. Three, they require cleaning and maintenance. Four, there's a real danger of theft and wanton damage." He'd reached his pinkie. "Five, don't you think that wealthy folk haven't already weighed up the pros and cons of such a venture and mostly decided against it?" He raised his other hand.

"All right, all right." I realised that my trip into fantasy land was getting me nowhere, and Jesús's lips were dry again. "Vicente, a wine for Jesús and beers for us. So, Jesús, what do you say to making some money and becoming the envy of your neighbours?"

He frowned. "Theft is a real danger in an isolated place like mine."

Juan patted the copy of Las Provincias on the bar. "In the papers you sometimes read about gangs stealing the panels and copper cables, especially from the larger installations."

"They should have security," I snapped. "Anyway, his roof is almost flat, so no-one will see them."

Juan grinned. "But he'll wish to boast about them, and as you know, in here even the walls have ears. Besides, shouldn't the panels be positioned at an angle?"

"Ideally, yes," I mumbled. "Thanks for your helpful advice, Juan."

Jesús's pre-lunch wine bonanza had made him pensive, but I feared that Juan's interference had put the kibosh on my second ever sale.

"Then again," the solar cynic said. "I'm sure an insurance policy wouldn't be too expensive."

I nodded. "That's true. I'll have to look into that."

"Then if one found the setup to be unprofitable or simply a nuisance, the panels might disappear or be damaged one dark night, eh?"

I gasped. "Would you do a thing like that, Juan?"

"Me? Of course not."

"The casita is insured," said Jesús. "So I'll call to ask them how much the panels would increase the price."

My lower jaw dropped, so I quickly hoisted it up. "Ye… yes, you do that. Shall I come to give you a quote later?"

He pushed away his empty glass and smacked his lips. "No, I must sleep on it first, Alan. One doesn't make such a big decision on the spur of the moment. Thanks for the drink. I'll call you if I decide to go ahead with it."

We watched him shamble out.

"A siesta for him today, I think," said Juan.

"Do you think he'll buy?"

"No."

"Oh."

"But he might, and the fact that a miser like him is even thinking about it can be considered a victory. Well done."

"Thanks, but you didn't help much."

"Oh, I think I did. People aren't stupid, you know, and I merely covered the questions that they're bound to ask."

I nodded. "That's true. I'm still a beginner, but I've already made a sale, touch wood." I tapped the bar.

"I'm glad, but I ask myself if being a salesman will really suit you."

"Why shouldn't it?"

"How many lies have you uttered so far today?"

"Lies?"

"Yes, and don't tell another one by denying it."

"Well, I wouldn't say I've *lied*, as such, although I may have made the odd, er… speculative statement."

"Are you looking for a field to buy near your sister's?"

"Well, not exactly, but as I was saying it, it began to seem like a good idea."

"I see. And do you have a spare hundred thousand or so with which to populate it with panels?"

"Ha, so much?"

He sighed. "Alan, fields are much, much bigger than roofs. I can draw a diagram if you like, but a little elementary arithmetic will tell you this. I advise you never to mention large projects like that again, as you'll just distract your customers from the subject at hand and they'll begin to doubt your sincerity, or sanity. Now, tell me, if I buy, for example, six square metres of panels, how long will it take me to recoup my investment if I use the house only at the weekends?"

I pursed my lips and stroked my chin. "Hmm, six square metres and five non-consuming days a week. Let me see, yes, it'd take you a... a few years."

"A few years?"

"Yes."

"Three? Seven? Twelve?"

"Yes."

"Yes what?"

"Er, somewhere between three and twelve, I'd say."

He groaned and pointed at the door. "Go home and study your products, Alan. That way you'll make far fewer of those speculative statements which you may live to regret, you not being a born rogue like Juanca and company. Hasta luego."

"Adiós, Juan." I asked Vicente for the bill and he plucked the amount from his agile mind.

"What? How the hell did I spend €32?"

"Jesús gave you most assistance, as the others only ordered a single drink." He went on to say that he'd seen far worse salesmen in action, but that I ought to heed Juan's advice and swot up on a few stats. I marvelled at his ability to rove up and down the bar serving drinks and still manage to follow every conversation. I paid up and said goodbye.

"Er, wouldn't you like to leave some of your leaflets here?"

"Oh, I hadn't thought of that. Do you think it'd be worthwhile?"

He sighed. "How many do you have?"

"Er." I held a thumb and finger about a centimetre apart. "This many."

He tutted. "And do they have your name and number on the back?"

I pulled out the one in my pocket. "Er, no."

"Oh, dear. Is your boss a total novice too?"

"He must be. He told me he's done a bit of selling, but he didn't say what," I said, as Fran had been rather vague about his working life to date.

"Do you see this white box on the back? Your name and number need to be here, loud and clear. Now give me thirty or so for starters."

I glanced around the emptying bar. "So many, for this lot?"

"What's wrong with my customers?"

I confessed that my perceived profile of my clientele was of middle-aged, middle-class folk, mostly foreigners, with money to spare and some semblance of a social conscience.

"I see. Like Jesús, you mean?"

I guffawed. "Course not. He's a one-off."

"A what?"

"A... an isolated case."

He sighed, shook his head, tutted repeatedly, then exhaled noisily using his lips to add a touch of vibrato to the high point of his scornful series of sounds. "You haven't a clue, have you?"

I shrugged and slumped against the bar, but during his subsequent discourse I gradually regained the confident posture I'd possessed on my arrival, although my chin remained at a suitably unassuming angle. After admitting that his bar wasn't the obvious place in which to push solar products, seeing as many of the blokes didn't possess country pads, he said I ought to know by now that news emanated from the place like radiation from Chernobyl – his words, not mine. He then expanded the radiation metaphor to include Inma's bar, Juanca's office, Cristóbal's car, Bernie's pocket, and any other places from where the word might be spread.

"Leaving them in supermarkets and suchlike is a waste of time, but you must use your contacts. Here, for instance, you're already in an unexpectedly strong position. If Jesús buys a few panels, he'll be harping on about them for the next six months, if not longer. Even if they fail to produce enough power for his heater, or the network pays him next to nothing, he'll never admit to that, so you simply must make him buy. That's my advice anyway."

I grinned and gripped the bar. "Wow, thanks, Vicente. I think I'm beginning to see the light; solar-powered, of course. Oh, but once he's slept on it I can't see him parting with so much money."

He smiled. "Give him a discount."

"Hmm, I suppose I could forgo my commission, just this once."

"Would you?"

"Yes. It's six percent."

His nose wrinkled. "Oh, you'll have to do better than that, Alan."

"Er, I can't afford to actually buy him the panels."

He sighed and reached for a pad. "About how much will they cost?"

"Oh, no more than two thousand for a little place like that."

"How fortunate that you told him two or three thousand." He wrote on the pad. "This is the normal price."

"€2750? Oh, I see… I think."

"So you offer him ten percent off, like so." He performed a lightening division. "€2475. He then moans, so you moan more loudly and after much agonising deliberation you offer him twenty percent off." Scribble, scribble. "€2200, an absolute bargain, but he moans again, so you whine and walk up and down and grasp your head, before offering him a ruinous twenty-five percent discount, just because he's been such a good friend to you and so on. That'll come to about two thousand, but you must calculate the initial figure more carefully." He dropped the pen. "He won't be able to resist such a tremendous bargain which only a man as astute as him could have achieved, but then you must make him swear not to breathe a word about the extra-special deal he's got."

"No, of course not. Er, why not, exactly?"

"So that the price he paid will become a great mystery and add another dimension to the hours and hours he'll spend gabbing about his panels." He rubbed the back of his neck and cringed. "I may live to regret giving you this advice, but it'll take his mind off even more tiresome subjects."

"Is he still clear of cancer?"

"Yes, but he goes on unleashing frightening statistics, given half a chance."

"Should I offer these… special discounts to others too?"

"Of course not. Anyone with a foot in the twenty-first century will compare the prices online."

"That's true."

I nipped back to the car to fetch the leaflets and he helped me to fill all the little white boxes, after which we sat down to lunch while his cook covered the bar. We talked about this and that, and after refusing payment he asked me if he could keep some of the leaflets.

"What do you mean? Of course you can, if you want."

He smiled. "Has it not occurred to you that I may be a potential customer?"

"Yes," I fibbed. "But I didn't want to talk shop during our meal."

He laughed. "Oh, what a poor liar you are, Alan! I have a small casita too, as you know, though I rarely get the chance to visit it." When he began to count his fingers I feared another Juan-style list of objections, but instead he reeled off a number of names. "…and my cousin Jorge," he said on the ninth digit. "So, in my extended family and my wife's there are nine country places, most of them modest, without solar power, but with mostly solvent owners." He raised his hands. "This is how things work in Spain, Alan, by word of mouth."

"Yes, I see."

"Though I imagine that any of them who may be interested will wish to see Jesús's installation, so call him tomorrow afternoon without fail, or better still, go to see him. I shall prepare the ground."

"I can't tell you how grateful I am, Vicente."

"Then don't." He pointed at the door. "Go forth and multiply your contacts."

"Yes, I will."

With so many things buzzing around in my head I decided not to visit any more chalets until the morrow, so I drove home to mug up on a few essential matters, not least the length of time it would take my lucky customers to recoup their investments. In my new catalogue I found a series of large, colourful graphs which I'd failed to notice before, and after perusing a few I was pleased to find that the cost of a typical installation could be recouped in as little as three years. Not quite believing the company's optimistic claims, I went online and searched for more objective statistics. On one apparently authoritative website I discovered that several factors had to be taken into account, such as the surface area, the orientation of the panels, one's level of consumption, the hours and intensity of sunlight, and a few more things that I couldn't quite understand. After inserting a few random variables for the Alicante Province I was relieved to see that more often than not the calculator stated that one's initial costs would be covered after four or five years, so I decided to quote that figure to my future clients.

Despite feeling slightly fatigued by all those numbers – maths never having been my strong point – I decided to spend another hour swotting up on the products that were soon to make us rich. On the company website I was delighted to see that for a small extra cost insurance was included, and on another site I read that the efficiency of solar panels had risen so much in the last few years that those installed a decade ago were considered practically obsolete.

"Ha, one-upmanship," I said aloud, before reading that in the same period prices had fallen by up to seventy percent. "Two-upmanship," I cried, deciding on the spot to make a point of targeting chalet owners whose neighbours possessed those laughably antiquated plaques which had cost them an arm and a leg.

"But I mustn't labour the point, or they might decide to wait for even cheaper prices," I muttered.

"Talking to yourself again, I see," Inma said in Spanish.

I slapped the laptop shut and hurried over to relieve her of a couple of shopping bags, before helping her out of her coat.

"You seem very pleased with yourself."

I smiled and shrugged, not wishing to start babbling right away. "A cup of tea, love?"

"Yes, please."

"Have you had a good day?"

"Not bad. Randi's come home."

"Ah, good. Anyway, you'll be pleased to hear that... what did you say?"

"Randi's come home, to Arvid."

"Hmm, so Bernie owes Cathy a euro."

"Is that all you can say? Are you not pleased for them?"

"Er, I don't know. Should I be? I mean, having led a sheltered life I've no experience of extra-marital affairs and their... aftermaths. Won't Arvid's jealousy ruin their attempt at reconciliation?"

She filled the kettle. "I assume they've discussed everything at length. Knowing Arvid and his cold, analytical mind, he'll have weighed things up objectively and decided that he's better off with her than without her."

"Speaking of analytical minds, I've been analy... but never mind my work for now, as your news is far more important," I said, in case it was, though I couldn't really see why.

She smiled. "She came to the bar this morning, looking very tanned and healthy. Her lover left Calpe a few weeks ago, you see, then Arvid went to visit her several times. At first they discussed divorce, partly because Randi wanted to return to Norway and needed a settlement to do so, but in the end he persuaded her to come back to him."

"I see." I wondered if their solar panels were already becoming obsolete and concluded that they probably weren't, as Cristóbal had once remarked that they'd cost the damn fool a fortune. "I see."

She filled the teapot. "I suppose it's no big deal to you, but it's great news for Rosa and me, as she'll be coming back to cook for us."

"Ah, so you'll be booting out the other girl, I suppose."

"Of course not. We wouldn't dream of it, although Randi's a far better cook than Alicia. No, Randi will just work part-time, and cover the holidays."

"I see." I wondered if Rosa and my good wife might consider installing solar panels at the bar. Sometimes one misses things which are right under one's nose, I mused.

Inma filled the mugs and added milk to mine. "You'll be pleased about that."

"Yes, I am. Er, what about?"

"About Randi covering the holidays."

I sipped. "I'm delighted for her."

She groaned. "Whatever has happened today has erased certain things from your mind."

"What? Oh... yes, I see. Well, quite frankly, after you've heard about my astounding debut you'll understand that me wast... spending time at the bar might cost us thousands."

"Rosa still insists on you fulfilling your promise though, and so do I."

"But why?"

"To broaden your life experience, and to entertain us, but don't worry, you won't have to do nearly as many hours as you would have if Randi hadn't come back."

"Good old Randi, and Arvid too. I do hope things work out for them."

She picked up her mug and headed for the sofa. "Right, come on, tell me all about your marvellous debut."

Twenty minutes later, having uttered not a word during my brutally honest discourse, she sat up straight and grasped her thumb.

I enfolded the offending hand. "Please don't do that, love. Just let me have it."

"Have what?"

"Give it to me straight from the shoulder," I said, indulging in a little linguistic humour before she battered me with the home truths which I sensed were about to head my way.

"I understand. Right, first of all, one swallow doesn't make a spring."

"Er, I think you mean a summer."

"Not in Spanish. Try to forget about that first lucky sale, if it happens, because projecting your future income from that alone is absurd, even for you. As for this idea you have that Jesús buying a few panels will cause an avalanche of orders, forget about that too, because it won't happen."

I frowned. "It might."

She shook her head, before explaining that with such an expensive product the mild interest to actual sale ratio would be extremely high.

"You mean low."

"I mean that for every ten expressions of interest you receive, only one of those people will really look into it, and may well end up buying elsewhere or simply putting it off."

I growled softly. "You seem to be set on quashing my hopes."

"Not at all. I just don't want you to expect great sales, then feel awfully disappointed. Let's hope that I'm being overly pessimistic."

"Yes, let's."

"Now, about these lies."

I flinched. "Not lies, just speculative statements, but never fear, because I'm now armed with solid... more solid statistics, and I mean to avoid mentioning fields full or panels and other irrelevancies, so my scope for lie... speculative statements will be much reduced."

"I hope so." She patted my hand. "Because by being your sincere, honest self you'll have a lot more chance of selling."

"Amen. So, how much do you think I'll have made by the end of the month?"

"Including your salary?"

I shrugged. "If you wish to include that pittance."

"You first."

"Well, bearing in mind your discouraging words, I'll reduce my previous estimate to–"

"Wait! Let's write our estimates on post-its, then at the end of the month we'll see who was nearest."

"All right." I went to fetch the pad. "How much shall we bet on it?"

"Oh, no more than a euro. You might not be able to afford to pay me more."

"Ha!" I took a post-it to the table and after much deliberation wrote down my figure, then folded it tightly. Inma, aware of my insatiable curiosity, got some sellotape and wrapped it around each slip several times.

"These can go into the bottom of the cornflakes box until the day of reckoning."

"All right. Er, I hope your desire to win isn't too strong, dear, because my main motivation is to be able to buy you a house with huge windows and your very own artist's studio."

On hearing these inspirational words she frowned almost imperceptibly for a fraction of a second, before illuminating the dingy room with a radiant smile. "You don't know what I've written. I'm quite hopeful really. I think Vicente's advice about making contacts is very wise. I believe that's the way forward in this venture, as in most others in Spain. Go on visiting chalets, but don't neglect those close at hand."

"All right. Oh, do you think I should do my best to sell to Jesús?"

"Yes, but without making a loss."

"All right. Ah, I must give you some leaflets to take to the bar, with my name and number on them."

"I took some today."

"Oh, with my name and number on them?"

"Yes, after I'd written them."

"You think of everything."
"I try."

6

The following morning, after realising the impossibility of unwrapping Inma's post-it without ruining it, I set off and drove towards Cathy and Bernie's house. I had a hunch that the rather windswept area to the west and south-west of there might provide me with rich pickings, or at least some pickings. I hadn't so much as mentioned my range of nifty wind turbines yet, and if I could shift them anywhere it would be over there, where the wind howled for days on end throughout the winter months. I suspected that the foreigners who lived there compared themselves to those hardy pioneers who had conquered the Wild West, because they were miles from the nearest town and the several tiny hamlets housed few permanent residents. As they were so self-sufficient, I surmised, they would surely be eager to increase their independence still further by generating their own power.

I soon found my conjecture to be correct, because of the first seven chalets I saw, three of them had hefty wedges of panels on their roofs. I also saw a small field of industrial-sized panels close by and another one in the distance, so it seemed clear that solar power already had a foothold in this rather dreary hinterland with many abandoned acres. After a twenty-minute, roughly circular recce I rejoined the first wide track and decided to call at a compact chalet between two larger, panel-bearing ones. When I stepped out of the car two savage dogs flew towards me, barking like mad. They scratched frantically at the gate, desperate to sink their teeth into me, and although I tried manfully to stare them down, their eyes expressed such terrifying bloodlust that I soon backed away, as one of the monsters was trying to wriggle through a gap in the metal fence. I'd just opened the car door when a stout lady waved from the porch, before ambling across the gravel towards me.

"Hello, there," she said in English. "Settle down, Millie!" she snapped at the larger of the two fiends. "Ooh, they do get excited when people come. What can I do for you?" she said through the gate.

"Er, I've come to speak to you about solar power."

She chuckled. "A Spanish chap came about that last week, but my husband soon sent him on his way. I mean, he couldn't even speak English very well."

"How remiss of him," I muttered, also keen to be on my way, as the other ravening beast was now trying to worm its way through a more distant section of fence.

"Gracie! Come here, you silly dog." She began to slide open the heavy gate.

"Er, they don't bite, do they?"

She smiled. "Of course not. Cockers are ever so friendly, especially bitches. Come and have a cup of tea. It's not often we get visitors."

By the time I reached a porch very much like Cathy and Bernie's – the house seemed to have been built along the same lines, probably by the same builder during those heady years leading up to the 2008 crash – the two hyperactive spaniels had removed most of the natural oils from my hands with their slobbery tongues, but I didn't flinch or slap the little pests, because I felt sure that a dog-hater would have zero chance of making a sale. Not that I hate them, but I'm yet to join the ever-increasing ranks of caninophiles. Nowadays even macho Spanish chaps are occasionally to be seen towing stylishly clipped pedigree pooches around town; men whose grandfathers wouldn't have allowed one past the threshold, preferring to house them in shacks and throw them scraps, but I digress.

The lady's husband – this couple will remain nameless and even pseudonym-less, for certain reasons of my own – shuffled out in his tatty slippers and looked me up and down in a not altogether endearing manner.

"Good morning. I'm Alan."

The flaccid, crimson-faced chap grunted. "What are you selling then?"

"Solar panels and wind turbines," I said tersely, quite happy to cut short my visit before tasting my cuppa, as time was money for a fellow like me and I was in no mood to suffer the slings and arrows of unpleasant expats.

"Do try to be civil," the lady said from inside. "I did invite him in, after all."

And you exercise a little forbearance, I said to myself, as a salesman's path is strewn with ignorant gits like this one, and who's to say some of them won't end up buying?

He grimaced and pointed to a cushioned wicker chair in the sun, before flopping into another. I admired the gravelly view until he deigned to address me.

"We've looked into panels, but I can't be bothered with all the fuss. We've got one of them almond shell stoves, so we don't use all that much leccy."

"Here we are," said the lady as she placed the tray on the table between us and occupied the third chair. "To be honest we're not sure if we'll be staying here for that long, are we, love?"

He shrugged. "That's up to you. I like it. No-one bothers us here." He glanced at me. "Or hardly anyone."

"It is quite isolated," I said.

"I'll say," she said, before stating that she'd prefer to have a few more people around and that as they were both nearing seventy she thought they ought to be nearer to a hospital, just in case. "A Belgian lady in the house past that next one fell and broke her arm last year and the ambulance couldn't find the place. Her husband had to go and search for it and it was over two hours before they picked her up. Just imagine being in agony for all that time."

The man then told me that were one of them to fall ill or have an accident, the other would arrange to meet the ambulance at the nearest hamlet. "So that sort of thing won't happen to us."

"Still, it's a worry… oh, would you like sugar, Alan?"

"No, thanks." Just then the mercantile side of my mind was pondering on how to make this most difficult of sales. The only thing that occurred to me was that a pretty set of panels would add value to the property, but instead of firing such a long shot I decided to shelve my spiel for the time being and give them some sage advice, because I'd begun to feel sorry for the lady, stuck out in the sticks with her grumpy spouse. Instead of saying straight out what I thought they should do, given that he had firmly ruled out a return to England, I decided to make up a little tale concerning myself and my missus, as with a stubborn so-and-so like him any direct suggestions would almost certainly be rejected out of hand.

So, I told them that although Inma and I loved living inland and would be staying in the area for the foreseeable, we would almost certainly retire to somewhere much nearer to the coast.

"We'll have to choose a good spot, of course, but it isn't all as built-up as folk imagine. Down there I'll have far more British people to talk to," I said without cringing. "And of course everything is that much more convenient, including healthcare and the airports."

She sighed. "I think we ought to do that."

"But it's too dear, except in dumps like Torrevieja," said the grump.

"Not necessarily. South of there the coast is generally less developed, and all the way down to Almería there are towns and villages where houses and apartments don't cost the earth. Águilas, for instance, where my wife's parents have a place, is a bustling town with plenty of affordable property." I drained my cup. "That's what we plan to do anyway," I fibbed, but I felt that my lie was as white as a bleached sheet and might go some way to convincing the selfish old sourpuss to pay heed to his wife, who wasn't a bad sort.

He proceeded to gaze at his soiled toenails through the holes in his slippers, so I just smiled and rubbed my hands together. This reminded me that they were in need of a good wash, so the lady soon led me into the kitchen, where she quietly thanked me for my moral support.

"You're welcome."

"Can you recommend a good estate agent?" she murmured.

After drying my hands I slipped Juanca's card from my wallet. "This man is the best," I had to admit. "But insist on a high price, especially at first, as you can always lower it later," I added, as the rogue sometimes preferred a swift sale, as do many of his peers.

"Thank you."

In the old days I'd have asked her to mention my name, of course, or even written it on the back of the card, but now that I was a purely solar-powered salesman I refrained from doing so. I even considered asking her to expressly avoid mentioning me, but felt that might be a bit over the top, so after a few friendly words with the now pensive husband, his wife escorted me to the gate.

"Thanks, Alan. You've been a big help. He just needs that extra little push to see reason and I think you may have given it to him."

"I hope so." I gazed at the second house along the track. "Do you think the Belgians would be interested in solar panels?"

"I suppose they might be." She sighed. "They're a nice couple, though a little unusual, but we hardly see them." She jerked her head towards the house. "He isn't fond of foreigners, you see."

"Ah, right. Anyway, give Juanc... Juan Carlos a call sometime. He speaks pretty good English."

"We will. Thanks again, Alan."

"My pleasure."

As I trundled along the track I felt mightily pleased with myself for having selflessly stuck my oar into their affairs, but on recalling the taped up post-its in the cornflakes box I realised that if I spent all my time dispensing pearls of wisdom I'd lose our bet, so on reaching the Belgians' big white chalet I jumped out and pressed the intercom button long and hard, hoping that in my upbeat state I'd radiate positivity and clinch a much-needed sale. The inevitable dog, which had been resting under an old Toyota jeep, ambled towards me, wagging its tail. It looked like an Alsatian crossed with a fox, so pointy were its ears, and I was about to allow it to sniff my hand when a loud voice made me jump.

"Nooo! It may bite you!" a tall, tanned, wiry man in his fifties bellowed in Spanish as he loped towards me. His receding frizzy grey hair was unkempt, as were his slightly outlandish clothes, which comprised a colourfully embroidered waistcoat, an off-white collarless shirt, ragged green jeans and dusty old sandals. On closer inspection I saw that his black-rimmed glasses were taped with plaster at one of the joints and he had a prominent incisor missing.

No sale, I thought, because the chalet had seen better days and its environs were cluttered with all kinds of junk, including a clapped out car under a ragged cover, a selection of sinks, toilets and bidets, a tangled mass of fishing tackle, a heap of rusty cages, and, of all things, an ancient twin-keyboard organ totally exposed to the elements.

"Hola," I said, striving to look unperturbed by this unsightly scene which I hadn't seen on my drive-past due to the high breeze-block wall. "I'm Alan. I'm... selling solar panels."

He grinned. "Come in and I'll show you mine." He glanced down at the placid dog and patted its head. "Buck, Alan es un amigo. Un amigo, eh?" he said in a better Spanish accent than mine. "He can be a little unpredictable as he was treated cruelly by his former owners," he said as he pulled open the gate. "Welcome to Ketumati, Alan."

When I glanced at the number on the gate he chuckled. "Ketumati is our private name for the house. It's a legendary place in Buddhist tradition, but I think Nina just liked the sound of it. I'm Lars." We shook hands. "I guess you're English."

"Yes."

"But you like to speak Spanish."

"Yes."

"Me too." He closed the gate and led me over the weedy, ungravelled ground and around the house, where I saw a small swimming pool full of clean water. Being an observant kind of fellow, he sensed my surprise. "We swim every morning, all year round."

"Ah, that's brave."

He shrugged his narrow shoulders. "It cleanses the body and soul before the day's activities begin. Nina! Where are you? Come and meet our visitor."

A tall, slim lady with shortish grey hair soon emerged from a large wooden shed beyond the pool. She wore faded blue jeans, a thick green sweater, and held an old violin in her hand.

A musician! I thought, suddenly remembering that I was one too.

"Nina, this is Alan, from England," he said in Spanish. "He's come to speak about solar panels."

She strode boldly towards me, took my hand, and planted a firm kiss on my right cheek. I made ready to exchange a second, but she'd back away.

She giggled. "Oh, sorry, Alan, my Flemish customs still prevail," she said in excellent English.

"Alan is one of those rare Englishmen who likes to speak Spanish," Lars said in that tongue.

"Muy bien. Spanish then."

I asked her if she played the violin, not as daft a question as it might sound, because I'd noticed that the strings were frayed and the body slightly cracked.

She giggled again and her blue eyes sparkled. "You might say that I play *with* it." She turned to Lars. "Shall we do the shots before we have a drink?"

He smiled. "Yes, then Alan can see the sort of lunatics he's stumbled upon. I'll get the cameras."

They seemed like youthful people in lithe middle-aged bodies and I found them quite beguiling. When Nina said that she assumed I'd come to sell solar panels rather than chat about them, I admitted that I had.

"Do you sell many?"

"I've just started."

She glanced up at the red-tiled roof. "Mm, maybe we should get some."

"Lars said you had some."

"Oh, they're just props. Come on, let's find a good place for the photographs."

When she took my hand and led me around a vegetable plot rather like mine after Álvaro had begun to collaborate, I ought to have been surprised by her familiarity, but I'd already realised they were unusual people and it didn't feel so odd. After the grumpy British brute and his long-suffering wife they felt like a breath of fresh air and I was disinclined to hurry off on my rounds.

"Do you think this old length of fence will make a good background, Alan?"

I looked from the violin to the rickety fence and back. "Er, I suppose so."

"Or perhaps he could shoot from low down and get in the sky. Oh, I've forgotten the bow." She handed me the decrepit instrument and hurried back to the shed. I'd shouldered the violin, if that's the expression, and begun to try a bit of pizzicato when Lars emerged from the house with a hefty old camera around his neck and another more modern one in his hand.

"Ah, so you're going to be my model today, Alan."

"Er…"

"Excellent. It'll make a change, though when I begin you'll wonder what the hell's going on, ha ha."

Nina returned and handed me the bow. "It's lacking the horsehair, but that won't matter."

"Gracias. Er, should I pretend to play it?"

Lars smiled. "Yes, with great brio." He handed the old camera – a Hasselblad, I noticed – to Nina and prepared the bulky Nikon. "I'm going to do a one-point-five second exposure."

"Oh, isn't that quite a long one?"

He sniggered as he lifted the camera to head height. "Begin to play."

I started quite slowly, sure that the image would be blurred.

"Con brio, Alan, por favor."

I threw back my head and sawed the naked bow across the strings, but didn't fail to see Lars press the button then move the camera through a rapid figure of eight movement until the shutter clicked. He looked at the rear screen and nodded, before approaching to show me the shot.

"It's all… swirly," I said, resorting to the English adjective, as the image was one big blur with a vague outline of my moving head and another of my arm and the violin.

Nina approached. "Hmm, not bad. Try another from lower down to capture the sky."

So, while I played on he crouched and repeated the figure of eight shot, before taking another half dozen, employing more random arm movements. He showed me the results.

"Interesting," I said truthfully.

"Which one do you like best?"

"Er, this one."

Nina peered at the screen. "Yes, it's quite good. This line from the corner leads into the main motif and… oh, but Alan must be wondering what all this is about."

"Is it a kind of abstract photography?"

"That's right," said Lars. "Now, after choosing the best image I normally take a couple of shots on the medium format camera. This allows for even bigger and better prints than with the modern one." He clicked a rear button on the Nikon. "The fourth one. OK, let's do it again."

"But weren't your movements random?"

He grinned. "Not exactly. I have a sequence, but of course no two images are the same, which is the beauty of our peculiar art, if you can call it that."

"I see."

"Others do it too, Alan," said Nina. "In fact it was when we saw an oriental woman doing a similar thing in front of the cathedral in Murcia that we decided to give it a try."

Lars chuckled. "But I believe we've taken it a stage further, as you'll see shortly. All right, play it again, Alan."

After he'd taken two shots with the film camera we headed into the house. Lars trotted off and Nina led me into a large sitting room with surprisingly conventional furniture, hundreds of books, and a lot of pictures on the walls, some of them almost as swirly as the recent photos.

I touched one lightly. "This is a painting."

"Yes, one of mine," she said. "I do a little abstract painting, but right now we're concentrating on the photography."

"I see."

"You may think, as many do, that painting is a superior art to setting a scene and moving a camera around, but... well, I won't bore you with my theories now."

"Oh, go ahead. Tell me, I mean. My wife also draws and paints, though not abstract, or not yet."

She told me that when painting, one's intentions are premeditated and that the random nature of their chosen mode of photography removed this all too human element. "One makes a final choice, of course, and one is effectively the author of the work, but to a great extent the deliberate and sometimes mistaken choices one makes while painting are eliminated, so in a sense it's a purer art form."

I pursed my lips and nodded. If I hadn't already grown to like the amiable couple I'd have thought this explanation a lot of poppycock.

She giggled. "You probably think it's a lot of nonsense."

I smiled. "No, not really."

"And what you're about to see next will confirm your suspicions that we're a real pair of oddballs, but we do what we choose to and bother no-one. Very few people have seen us in action, you know, as we aren't immune to feeling ridiculed, but Lars must have liked the look of you, as I do."

I blushed lightly.

"Would you like tea, or another kind of infusion? We only have decaf coffee, as the real thing makes Lars too excited, then he goes out and brings back a load more rubbish."

Reminded of all their props outside, I took another look at the walls. "I can't see any of the abstract photos here."

"No, not yet, but we'll show you some."

Lars appeared, wafting a large photograph in the air. "Come and see what we do, Alan."

"To drink, Alan?"

"Tea, please."

Lars led me along a passage and into a biggish room containing several machines and many shelves full of books and files, plus a few boxes and miscellaneous objects scattered around. He flicked the photo that he'd just printed and pointed at the biggest machine.

"Have a guess what that's for."

"Er, some kind of printer?"

"I'll give you a clue." He held up the photo in which I featured. "What's the best thing we could do with something like this?"

"Er… oh, frame it?"

"No, chop it up, ha ha." He handed me the photo, before taking a card and pulling off a transparent layer. After carefully sticking the photo onto the card he placed it between some metal pegs on the platform and lowered a perspex cover, before pressing a foot pedal which moved the card slowly through the centre of the machine and onto the other part of the platform. He lifted the perspex and handed me the card. "Voilà."

I held it up and a bit fell off. "Ooh, it's a jigsaw puzzle!"

"Sí, un rompecabezas original con 250 piezas. Unique in the world." He picked up and replaced the fallen piece, before slipping the still stiff puzzle into an A4 sized envelope and handing it to me. "For you, Alan."

"Oh, gracias."

"I'll print you another photo, in case you actually want to do the puzzle."

"Oh, yes, my wife Inma and I will certainly do it."

He tittered. "They aren't easy, which is why some jigsaw aficionados like them."

"Oh, so do you sell them?"

"Yes, a few, but not the ones from this machine. These are just samples we make to see how they turn out. When we think we have a good one we send the file or the negative to a company back in Belgium and they produce bigger puzzles, usually with a thousand pieces. I think I have a couple here somewhere." After rummaging around for a while he handed me a box.

I perused the swirly, vividly coloured photo. "Oh, this is the organ and… something else."

"Yes, I crouched behind the organ and moved two small cages around. I think Nina's technique is better than mine." He pulled another puzzle from a box. "This is one of hers too."

I saw a swirling white object before a shiny background. "What's in this?"

"A bidet suspended on fishing line, with a solar panel behind." He smiled and shook his head. "When one explains these images the whole thing sounds quite absurd, but to us it seems no less worthwhile an activity than the more usual things that people do." He shrugged. "While other retired folk cultivate a garden or socialise or simply laze around in the sun, we do this and other more or less outlandish things."

"Chicos, come and get your drinks!" Nina hollered, so we went to join her.

While perusing the swirling solar panel photo I'd briefly remembered my morning's mission, but as we chatted I soon forgot about it again. In their previous lives Lars had worked as a merchant banker in Brussels, Buenos Aires and Frankfurt, while Nina had sold industrial diamonds all over the world. They'd felt burnt out by their mid-forties, but had soldiered on for another few years in order to amass enough money to do what the hell they liked for the rest of their lives. After travelling extensively, the 2008 crisis had clipped their wings a bit, so they'd moved to Spain a year later and snapped up the chalet for a song.

"We felt that we'd travelled enough for the time being," said Lars after Nina had told me most of the story. "And although we're quite wealthy again now, we feel no compulsion to move on just yet, though we think we might like to end our days in India."

"Why India?"

"Because of the strong spiritual element which one can still find there, away from the cities," said Nina. "We'd try to learn Hindi or whichever language they spoke where we settled." She giggled. "I could see us inviting some Sadhus, the travelling holy men, to stay with us. We'd try to find enlightenment through them, but it may never happen. More tea?"

"Sí, gracias. So do you do meditation and things?"

"We try," said Lars. "Nina has more success than me. I still feel somewhat corrupted or… corroded by the life I used to lead and find it hard to concentrate on one thing for long. One minute I'll be floating in the pool, gazing up at the stars on a summer's night, and the next I'll be online, checking our investments."

Nina giggled. "We're both just dilettantes really, trying to amuse ourselves and hoping to achieve a more lasting fulfilment one day. Family ties bind us to Europe right now, as our grandchildren are just ten and seven, so we find ourselves on those awful aeroplanes, which we used to use so much, far more often than we otherwise would."

Lars nodded. "Our son is a very conventional person, you see, as we used to be, and he refuses to bring the children to this rubbish dump, as he calls it." He pointed to the gap in his teeth. "When we're at their house near Brussels I must always wear my denture and my finest clothes. He calls us hypocrites, me especially, for making a lot of money in an unethical manner, then becoming silly hippies in our old age."

"He's a doctor and very proud of his calling," said Nina. "Anyway, enough about us."

So I gave them a potted history of my mostly lazy life, before admitting that filthy lucre had become uppermost in my mind since we'd decided to sell the cave house. "Thus the solar panel sales, and wind turbines too, although I doubt I'll sell many of them."

Lars tutted. "And here we are, keeping you from your work."

"We should get some solar panels really," said Nina.

"Did a Spanish salesman not call last week?" I asked.

She giggled. "No, salesmen have a habit of passing us by, once they've looked through the gate."

I asked them if they knew many people in the area.

"Not up here, but down on the coast we have a few like-minded friends."

Lars screwed his finger into his temple. "Half-crazy folk like us, especially Gerard, a German guy in Altea who paints ceramics and smokes a lot of pot."

"Which we don't do," said Nina. "Or drink much either." She giggled yet again. "We feel no need for any mind-changing substances."

Lars gritted his teeth. "Although sometimes I could kill for a good strong coffee."

She gave him a shove. "I've told you, for every car-load of stuff you take to the tip in Jumilla you can have one."

I remembered something. "Oh, Nina, the neighbours told me you broke your arm not long ago."

"Yes, I fell off the wall as I was waving two fishing rods."

Lars stroked her left arm. "I got a good shot, but we didn't use it, poor girl."

I couldn't resist asking them about the couple, but they expressed no real opinion. Lars told me they'd invited a few people who they'd got chatting to in the nearby towns to pay them a visit, but had yet to receive any.

"Some may have come, but, like the salespeople, I believe they'll have taken a look through the gate and hurried away." He shrugged. "Conventional people bore us anyway, and we're quite self-sufficient here."

Feeling proud to be considered a not wholly conventional person, I told them about our recent sabbatical in Asturias. "…so it was a refreshing change and we began to do new things, but this year we must work hard."

"We'll have a think about panels, won't we, Lars?"

"Yes, and..." He checked that my cup was empty. "Let's go out."

On stepping outside Lars loped off and after striding around their sloping and mostly scrubby land – about half the size of a smallish soccer pitch – he hailed us from near the northernmost point. "It's always windiest up here," he yelled. "Come and feel the breeze."

We joined him and from that spot near the top of a shallow ridge I remarked that it must really blow on windy days.

"Yes, we get some proper gales out here and very few still days," he said. "How about a little wind turbine, Nina?"

"Hmm, yes, it might look nice up here."

"And make a great backdrop for our photos."

I refrained from rubbing my chilly hands together. "I'm not sure how much power a turbine would generate. To be honest I haven't studied them much, as I don't expect to sell many, but I can try to come up with some figures if you like."

Lars licked a finger and held it up. "It's got to be the best place in the whole area. Yes, we'd like to have a look at some."

"Er, I think I've left the turbine brochures at home."

Nina giggled. "Even better. Then you'll have to come back to see us."

I smiled. "I'd like that."

Nina, Lars and the supremely discreet Alsatian-fox cross accompanied me out to my car and I agreed to return the following morning, before shuffling from foot to foot and scratching my head.

"I wasn't really hoping to make a sale, you know. It's been great to meet you and... well, don't feel that you have to buy anything."

Nina laughed loudly this time. "Oh, I'd have shifted few diamonds if I'd had that attitude, Alan."

"And the bank would soon have sacked me if I hadn't been a scheming devil when I had to be." He put his arm around me. "Make no mistake, Alan, we haven't always been whimsical old fools, messing around with cameras and piles of junk. We were real go-getters for a long time, always lusting after another dollar."

"You aren't so old," was all I could think of to say.

"I'm sixty-three and he's a year older," said Nina.

"You look younger."

"Now, maybe," said Lars. "But at fifty I looked like a walking corpse." He pulled down the skin under his eyes and leered at me. "I'd been taking amphetamines to keep going during those last few years, then pills to make me sleep."

Nina stroked his arm. "We bailed out before he seriously damaged his health." She pointed through the gate. "And look at us now, the envy of folk for miles around."

On this light-hearted note I took my leave and soon found myself making a beeline for Inma's bar, but before entering the hamlet I took a right, because I felt a serious bout of babbling coming on and the bar would be getting busy, so I went to my sister's to babble to them instead. Cathy was out and by the time I reached Bernie on the allotment I'd calmed down and decided to keep my Belgian pals' idiosyncrasies to myself for the time being. Me being a highly impressionable person, their approach to life had sent all sorts of obscure messages to my recently placid and pragmatic brain, but as I had no idea how to articulate them I'd be well-advised to only disclose the immense stroke of luck I appeared to have had. So it was that after relating my visit to the grump and his wife, I added that I'd seen a Belgian couple who would almost certainly be buying a wind turbine.

He jabbed his hoe into the loose and weedless earth. "Well done, mate, especially with the Brits."

"Why the Brits?"

"Because if they sell through Juanca you'll get your cut, of course."

I raised my chin. "I swear that it never crossed my mind. My motives were purely altruistic."

"Yeah, right. Call the bugger anyway in case they go to see him."

"I'll do no such thing," I said, feeling fairly sure that the lady would mention the tall, considerate man who had helped to end her rural isolation. "Do you know the Belgians couple who live down that way, or know of them?"

"Nope. How's the goldmine?"

"What?"

"Zefe."

"Behaving, I think, since Álvaro's threat."

He shook his head and clucked like the hens he was thinking of buying, or so Cathy had told me on the phone. "Risky move that. If old Alv knows on which side his bread's buttered he'll be as well to cater to Zefe's every whim. If he boots him back to his flat, he might hobble round to the lawyer's and draw up another will, and then where will we be?"

"*We?*"

He grasped both my arms just above the elbows and gazed greedily into my eyes. "The three of us came to Spain as a team, remember? All for one and one for all, eh?" He released me from his iron grip, having become a good deal stronger since beginning to pilot his unwieldy old tractor almost every day. "And you stay in his good books too. You never know, if he pops his clogs soon you might end up with a better house than you expected."

"Oh, dear, I see gold fever is still coursing through your veins."

"Some of those guys in Brazil made a bloody fortune, you know. I've been reading about that mine, in Portuguese."

"Muito bem."

"With a little help from the translation tool. Yeah." He swept his arm around in an almost full circle. "We'll be able to buy all this up, including the Norwegians' place." He chuckled. "I'm only kidding really, but all landowners dream of greater acreage."

"Oh, how are Arvid and Randi? I'd forgotten she was back."

He gazed across the field of almond trees. "They're thinking of selling up and going back home, or so I've heard on the grapevine." He sighed. "Oh, I'd love to buy the place, and that field, then I'd have the beginnings of a proper ranch. Ha, I could turn their house into stables and breed horses." He tipped back his old straw hat and gave me one of his cunning Eli Wallach-type looks. "Then again, you two could buy it."

"This grapevine must work bloody fast, Bernie, because Inma hasn't said a word about it."

"Oh, you know how she hates gossip, and that's all it is. You staying for lunch? Cathy'll be back soon, I hope, 'cause I'm starving."

I declined the invitation, because night would fall not long after six and I wanted to pay a few more visits rather than spend the afternoon gossiping.

7

On arriving home I made a butty and was reading about abstract photography online when my phone rang. I grinned on seeing Jesús's name, but refrained from answering until the jingly tone began to annoy me.

"Sí," I barked.

"Are you coming round, or what?"

I smiled. "Too busy today, I'm afraid."

"Vicente said you would."

"Ah."

"We've been talking and I'm interes... a bit curious about this solar panel business. I'm not saying I'll buy, mind you, but I'd like to talk prices and whatnot."

"Hmm, let me see." I lowered my phone and rustled a nearby notepad. "This afternoon I've got to see an English couple who are placing a big order, and a Belgian couple who want a huge wind turbine." More rustling. "Hmm, and a Spanish family up towards Yecla who want to power a large finca solely with solar panels," I added in a mendacious attempt to appeal to his patriotic instincts. "So you see, Jesús, I can't really spare the time to come out there to chat about some tiny setup that you might not even buy."

"Suit yourself."

"I'll try my best to come over sometime tomorrow, but my phone never stops ringing and I can't promise anything." I covered my mouth and sniggered.

"You aren't the only solar panel merchant around, you know."

"I know. All right, I promise to come tomorrow."

He grunted goodbye and hung up. Before setting off to find some new customers I remembered to check my emails and found a recent one from the Chippenham couple. On reading that after thinking it over they'd decided to go for a 5000W kit in the end, as it made no sense to do things by halves, I clenched my fist and punched the air. Then I read the next sentence:

However, before committing ourselves we really want to see an installation that's already working, so please let us know when you can take us to see one.

I remembered to unclench my fist before striking my forehead, then I grabbed my phone.

"Jesús," I crooned.

"What is it now?"

"I think I can fit you in after all," I said, before apologising for having allowed my success to go to my head. "It's all go at the moment, you see, but you are a good friend, after all, and one must get one's priorities right."

"I'll put some coffee on," he said, then hung up.

I gave Fran a quick call, then jumped in the car.

Twenty minutes later I was entering the familiar casita and over coffee we opened negotiations. Fortunately Vicente must have done some serious softening up work that morning, because Jesús soon told me to cut the crap and quote my very best price.

"Because I'm going to have some panels, and do you know why?"

"Why?"

"Because this morning young Diego pointed out that solar panels were a long-term investment."

"I see. Was he sober?"

"Perfectly. Cristóbal has finally landed a big job."

"I'm glad," I said sincerely, because I couldn't even offer him work installing the panels, as the specialists would be doing that.

"Anyway, he mentioned long-term investment in a tone which suggested it might not be worth my while."

"Oh."

"I'm only seventy-one, for God's sake!"

"Yes, but... but..." I was loath to mention the C-word, as it might open the floodgates and delay the deal which I simply had to seal right away.

"Oh, I know I've had prostate cancer, but I'm all clear now, and although statistics suggest that I may be less likely to reach a great age than I was before, I resented his insinuation that I might drop dead any minute."

"Hmm, but your, er... slight preoccupation with your illness may have given the impression that you didn't expect to be around for long."

He stamped on the concrete floor. "Bah, those fools mistake statistics for flesh and blood and a beating heart! It's all about the will to live, you see. If you lose it, statistics say... well, never mind statistics. Vicente told me that I'll make no money from the panels for about four years. Is that right?"

"About that, yes."

"So, I can't possibly weaken during that time, because you know what a frugal man I am, don't you?"

"Yes."

"That'll take me to seventy-five, or maybe seventy-six, because I suppose it'll take a while to install the panels."

"Not necessarily. In fact, if we reach an agreement this afternoo–"

"So, at seventy-five or six I'll begin to make some money from the sunlight." His beady eyes narrowed. "Do you seriously think a man like me will contemplate snuffing it once that starts to happen?"

I smiled. "No, I don't suppose so."

"So, you see, my already tremendous will to live will be strengthened still more by these newfangled gizmos."

On witnessing his unprecedentedly upbeat state, my innate salesmanship kicked in and I pointed out that his profits from the half dozen panels which would fit on his south-east-facing roof would be unlikely to make him rich. "It's a small area, you see. On the other hand, if you were to use your least productive field instead, then you could make some serious money."

He scowled.

"Yes, I know the initial outlay would also be high, but one reaps what one sows."

"Are you suggesting that any of my fields aren't productive?"

"Oh, no…"

"Or that generations of my forebears haven't known how best to exploit the soil under their feet?"

"No, no." Juan had told me that his grandfather had bought the land cheap from a dipsomaniacal squire. "But you know you aren't all that fond of growing vegetables anyway. Assign part of that field to panels and you'll reap rewards the like of which your forbears couldn't even have dreamed of." I raised my hands towards the smoke-stained ceiling. "God's bounty will reward your investment, and you'll be the envy of everyone in the area."

"Don't be blasphemous. You can forget that idea anyway." He sighed. "I sometimes think you don't understand me at all, Alan."

"I try."

"Don't you see that the panels will be merely a symbolic gesture? An appeal to God, if you like." He crossed himself. "Telling Him that I'd like to stick around for a while longer, no matter what the statist... anyway, enough chatter. Name your best price."

"Two thousand, including IVA and installation and insurance."

"And a guarantee?"

"Yes, a ten-year mechanical guarantee and a twenty-five-year energy production guarantee."

He grinned. "By which time I'll be ninety-six, or seven."

"Definitely ninety-six, because the one condition attached to my super-special price is that you must buy them right away," I said, before confessing that I simply had to have a set of panels up and running as soon as was humanly possible. "Because some people may be coming to see them."

"All right, I'll give you a cheque tomorrow."

I whipped out my unblemished order book. "Sign here."

When he'd signed and gone off to plough his weedless field of olive trees I called Fran. He told me he'd already made two sales, but given the urgency of my request he promised to get the company to give Jesús's life-lengthening installation top priority. I then enthused about the English couple's 5000W kit and the Belgians' yet to be determined wind turbine.

The unflappable fellow chuckled. "That's great, but little by little, Alan. Right now we're laying the groundwork for future sales, which I'm sure will grow once word gets around that the best company in Spain is finally operating in our area."

"All right, Fran."

"But remember not to neglect potential Spanish customers. Both my sales were to Spaniards, and while I understand that you'll have more affinity with fellow foreigners, the bulk of our market is the native population, after all."

"Sí, Fran. I'll go to find some right away."

He laughed. "It'll be dark before long. Go home and relax, and congratulations on your first sale."

"Gracias, Fran."

Jesús had done ploughing for the day, so after another chinwag with my unlikely saviour I headed for home. After emailing his details to Fran I spent a long time mulling over my encounter with the Belgians.

When Inma arrived at nine I popped the covered dish she'd brought into the microwave, took a lovingly crafted salad from the fridge, and opened a bottle of white wine.

My slightly fatigued wife smiled. "I take it you've had a good day, dear?"

"Yes, not bad, but I won't bore you with my work." I shrugged. "It isn't the be-all and end-all, after all."

The microwave pinged and we were soon tucking into Randi's delicious lamb stew.

"You're free tomorrow, I believe," I said.

"Yes, but I suppose you'll have to work."

"I'm afraid so, but that'll give you an opportunity to get your paints out."

She sighed. "Yes, I suppose so, but... oh, I feel so little inspiration just now. It isn't the same without having the sea to paint. I love painting water, you see, and there aren't even any decent rivers or reservoirs around here, let alone a lake."

"Then we'll go to the seaside on Sunday."

"That would be lovely."

"Tomorrow you'd better get plenty of practice, so you'll be, er... loosened up."

"All right, but you'll get bored on Sunday while I'm painting."

I tutted softly. "Not at all. I'll go for a walk and… maybe take a few photos."

"On that old phone of yours? It's only got about three pixels."

"Ha, yes, but no. I'm going to buy a decent digital camera. Nothing too expensive, just something to, er… express myself with. My keyboard playing's all very well, but I'm really only reproducing other people's songs, and slowly," I said, as my musical learning curve was proving to be a very shallow one, in the sense that it was taking its time to curve upwards at all, although the fact that I was playing for no more than twenty minutes a day may have had some bearing on my lack of progress.

I cleared my throat. "I might also begin to do a little drawing again."

She laughed. "Again? No sooner had you begun than you quietly gave it up."

"Yes, well, I believe I was approaching it the wrong way and not giving my imagination, er… free rein. I may draw in a slightly more (mumbled word) way."

"What?"

"In a slightly more abstract way."

Her tinkly laughter filled the room. "Oh, Alan, but you disliked the abstract work in the Centro Botín in Santander. What was it? Ah, yes, 'Some of this modern stuff is all right, but I hope you'll master the true art of painting rather than daubing canvases like a child of five,' was what you said, more or less."

"I was paying more attention to the architecture. Hmm, architecture, that might be interesting…" I slapped the table. "Anyway, never mind me. You've got to get back into your painting or our sabbatical will end up being a mere parenthesis in our lives of unending toil. We returned from the north feeling that we'd unleashed our creative powers, and look at us now. You scarcely picking up a brush or a pencil and me lazily playing the same infantile songs."

"But…"

"You slaving away at the bar, and me getting all excited about selling a few lousy panels. Oh, because of this damned house we have to buy we'll end up selling our souls to Mammon!" I downed half a glass of wine and slumped back in my chair.

Inma laid down her spoon, sipped her wine, and clasped her hands. "Now you're going to tell me exactly what happened to you today."

"I sold a few panels to Jesús," I muttered.

"What else?"

"I gave an English couple some sound advice."

"What else?"

I told her about the Chippenham couple's email and my rapid response.

"Muy bien. What else?"

"Oh, I may be selling a wind turbine to another couple, a Bel… Belgian couple."

She wrinkled her nose and sniffed like an especially astute bloodhound. "Now I sense that we're getting closer to the cause of your, er… mental disturbance."

"I am *not* mentally disturbed."

"Then I'll put it another way. Something that someone said to you today has affected your brain. In the space of a few hours you've changed from being a single-minded solar salesman to a flighty, unsettled individual who desperately needs to find an outlet for his creative urges."

"Nonsense," I mumbled.

"Tell me about the Belgians."

So I did, at some length, and in a fairly objective manner, though I did airbrush out much of the junk and stress the commercial nature of their abstract jigsaw project, despite Lars having told me that it was scarcely profitable.

"So you see, they worked really hard for years and now they do as they please. They begin each day with a refreshing bathe and then follow the creative dictates of their open minds. They take artistic photographs, or paint, or... or do any number of creative things," I said, wishing I'd asked them what they'd got up to before the swirly photography had occurred to them. "Meeting them has merely underlined how we've lost our way in the short time since we returned, that's all."

"I see," she said, before finishing her stew in a leisurely and thoughtful manner, so I did likewise while waiting for her to opine on the matter. Instead, after placing the plates in the sink and fetching some fruit, she asked me about the English couple I'd seen.

I shrugged. "They're irrelevant. Just a grumpy guy and his poor old wife who I advised to go to live at the seaside. Lars and Nina are far more interesting."

"Yes, well, never mind them for now. What you've told me explains your restless state, so I'm no longer concerned about them. I think you gave the English folk some excellent advice."

I shrugged modestly. "Yes, I believe I did."

"And not only because she'll be able to socialise more on the coast, but because their whole perspective will change. Where they live now the countryside is drab and uninspiring, but seeing the sea every day may well open their minds, even his, rather like these Belgians have opened yours. More wine?"

"Just a drop." I noticed a distinctly dreamy look in her eyes. "Yes, we'll definitely go to the coast on Sunday. We should go more often really."

She sighed. "Yes, but it's so far away."

"Only an hour."

"Yes, to the nearest place, with no cliffs or anything else interesting to paint."

"But you like Santa Pola, and one can see Tabarca from there."

She scoffed. "A flat featureless little island that even you could draw." She traced a single line on the tablecloth. "Like so."

"Then we'll go further afield." I reached over and squeezed her hand. "Wherever you wish, cariño."

"Gracias, and I will paint a little tomorrow, but I fear that I'm beating around the bush, rather like you often tend to do, instead of telling you what's really on my mind."

I gulped. "What is it?"

She smiled and began to peel an apple. "Have my unsubtle hints not given you a clue? Can't you guess?"

I also grasped an apple and a knife, hoping to produce a single length of peel as she invariably did. "Er, I could, but I'd rather not."

"Yes, you're right. I'll tell you straight, but you'd better put the knife down."

I complied, wondering if the fateful moment had finally arrived. Since we'd returned from Asturias I'd inflicted the irritating Zefe on her, got into a tiresome tizzy about the hotel sale, rattled on endlessly about the solar panel scheme, then suddenly, out of the blue, I'd performed a perfectly ridiculous volte-face and begun to blather about my creative inquietude, provoked solely by a Belgian chap waving a camera around. At first she'd thought that a trip to the seaside might clear the air, but on reflection she'd decided to lay her cards on the table, and I had an inkling that one might be my P45. And who could blame her? Still beautiful at forty-six she had time to find herself a sane, sensible, well-rounded man who could provide for her, instead of being at the mercy of a twittering twerp like me.

"Yes, tell me straight, Inma."

"In the not too distant future I'd like to live by the sea."

I nodded twice then bowed my head. Of course, that made sense. Better to make a clean break and start life afresh elsewhere. Once she had the money from her cave house she could buy an apartment somewhere pleasant and after hurling her wedding ring into the sea she'd step out and soon meet a wealthy, cosmopolitan chap who would whisk her off her feet and offer her a life somewhat like her old friend Susana's, with a huge chalet and a summer retreat. She knew that I'd be all right, of course, as I'd simply move back into my room at my sister's, where I'd spend the remainder of my days scrolling through lists of coins and pining for my lost love…

I am exaggerating ever so slightly, of course, but for some reason I really did fear that she was becoming fed up of my capricious ways. Like the English lady I'd felt sorry for, perhaps she believed that in a bustling coastal place she wouldn't be immured between four walls – or partly underground, as at present – with such a changeable chump and would be able to nip to a cafe whenever I began to babble, blather, bullshit, or fall into her arms after my latest distressing episode.

"Alan?"

"Hmm?"

"I don't mean any time soon, so don't start worrying about my job or your panel sales or whatever."

Upon feeling my hair being ruffled, I slowly raised my head. "Ah."

She giggled. "That's just like you to start fretting about practicalities right away. No, I'm talking about five or even ten years from now, though to be honest I'd prefer to go sooner rather than later."

I smiled and nodded, striving to keep my sense of relief to myself. If she thought she could handle five more years holed up with me, maybe my fears were unfounded after all.

"I know this may come as a surprise to you, but since Asturias I've found myself pining for the sea more and more. I guess it's only natural after the lovely time we had, but I think it's more than that. I've spent most of my summers in Águilas since I was a child, and I lived in Alicante for years, so… well, all this nattering is really only leading to one simple proposal."

"And what's that?"

"I think we should look for a house to rent rather than buy one."

"Hmm, right, yes, OK… but why didn't you just say that, love?"

She tittered. "Oh, dear, I must be becoming more like you, unable to come to the point. They do say that couples grow to resemble each other, don't they?"

I puffed out my cheeks and exhaled. "Then let's just hope that your stronger, more stable character prevails."

"Let's finish our meal."

When I managed to produce a single strip of apple peel I thought it a good omen, and over our decaf I opined that this rental idea seemed to have lifted a weight from my mind. I rested my chin on my hand and rocked it up and down.

"In fact my head already feels lighter. I do… did so want to find the best possible house for you and knew that it'd cost a lot more than we have to spend, so my desire to sell panels became almost obsessive."

"Yes, until the Belgians turned your head."

I flapped my hand. "Just a hiccup. Tomorrow I'd have been out there again, racing from chalet to chalet like a man possessed, the tension rising as I reached each gate – and not because of the dogs – knowing that each sale might buy you another window or a couple more square metres. I'd have approached the owners, my heart beating like a hammer, praying that they'd buy and probably fluffing the sale through being too eager to amass more and more filthy lucre. All that, plus my tendency to count my sales before they're hatched, would soon have taken its toll, ageing me prematurely, so that when we did finally acquire our dream home I'd be a mere husk of a man, drooling in a rocking chair and... that sort of thing," I said, becoming aware as I ranted that I'd hardly blazed much of a trail so far, thus the attempt to turn an initially sincere speech into a spot of self-mockery.

Inma smiled. "Yes, and I think that if you go at your own speed, however slowly that is, you'll probably sell more anyway. Just imagine that you're selling coins again."

"Yes, er..." I remembered the final, self-pitying bit of my calamitous conjectures. "But what have coins got to do with it?"

"Just a moment." She entered the depths of the cave and soon emerged with the slim plastic box containing my very finest coins.

I gasped. "How did you find that?"

The other day when I was mopping I lifted a loose tile and there it was. I thought you might have forgotten where you'd hidden them."

"Ha, not likely. I scraped out the hole especially, not to hide them from you, dear, but us numismatists are like magpies." I undid the clips. "Ha, let's have a look at my precious treasures." On opening the lid I rubbed my eyes, then patted the foam between the special plastic pouches, then emitted a plaintive wail. "Oh, it's all damp!" I grasped my 'Very Fine' William IV sovereign (second bust) and peered at it, before checking my 'Good' (i.e. worn) but still valuable Charles II half-crown (third bust), my 'Extremely Fine' George III crown, and the other nine coins. "Damn it, they've got a bit mouldy."

"Yes, I was going to polish them for you with some metal cleaner I found in the cupboard."

I slapped the lid shut and clasped the box to my chest. "Oh, my God! That would've been disastrous. I mean, the patina! You could have halved their value in a matter of minutes."

"I was joking. You told me all about coin care when you used to be interested in them."

I patted my patients. "I still am, in these beauties anyway." I opened the box and pulled out the damp foam. "A little distilled water is all they need, and a new hiding place."

She smiled. "How much are they worth?"

"Oh, it's hard to say. It depends on the market, you know, and I'm a bit out of touch. Maybe eight or ten... oh, do you want me to sell them?"

"No, but if you've lost interest, you might as well. There's no sense in keeping things of such value when the money would be safer in the bank. I'll get the distilled water."

I went into the cave to fetch the rest of my collection, all hidden in more sensible places, like under my undies and in the pockets of my seldom worn jackets. After Inma had cleared the table I spread them out and feasted my eyes on centuries of numismatic history.

"It's the first time I've looked at them all for a long time. Do you know, I can remember the circumstances of almost every purchase. Oh, the time I spent putting this collection together! Look at this humble Victorian penny. I stayed up half the night to place my decisive bid, because it was in Australia. This shilling was a real bargain at a car boot sale, while I paid over the odds for this farthing, because I'd fallen in love with it." I scratched my head. "Strange as that may sound."

"Shall I clean these mouldy ones?"

"No, dear." I relieved her of the bottle. "You may rub too hard. So, er... why did you... that is, did you sort of choose your moment to reveal my coins' lamentable state?"

"In order to create the greatest impact? In a way, though I'd have shown you soon anyway. What do you think, now that you see them all together?"

"Er, a certain fondness, I suppose."

"Anything else?"

"Like what?"

"Oh, I don't know, a desire to buy more and maybe sell a few that don't mean much to you."

"Hmm, I suppose so. These two George II halfpennies are pretty similar, for instance. I could sell one of those and buy a farthing or something." I took my box of favourites and closed it, minus the offending foam. "I'll clean these tomorrow in the daylight." I smiled. "So, Inma dear, what's the lesson I'm meant to learn from this spontaneous coin festival?"

She patted my hand. "I'll let you decide for yourself."

"Yes. I'll put these away."

Me being me, however, I couldn't just sleep on the evening's events, and later in bed I had to attempt to reach some sort of conclusion.

"Yes, a well-balanced life is best, so I'll sell some solar stuff, shift a few coins, keep my eyes open for other opportunities, look for a house to rent, play the keyboard and sing a bit, and maybe, just maybe, try to expand my creative horizons by trying something new."

"Yes, Alan."

"*And* we must really start to make the most of our free time. From now on, when you're free I will be too, and we'll shoot off down to the seaside whenever you wish."

She yawned. "Sí."

I twiddled my thumbs on the duvet. "Hmm, five to ten years, you said, but you prefer five, and so do I. Yes, so what we need is a Five Year Plan, a bit like Roosevelt had, or was it Stalin?"

She moaned contentedly, I think. "Whoever it was, I don't want one."

"No, come to think of it, it was Stalin, so I don't want one either. Ha, a New Deal then, and the deal is that we rent cheap and save loads of money, ha ha."

"Yes. Now let's go to sleep."

I kissed her tenderly and turned off my bedside light. On hearing her sigh of satisfaction I closed my eyes, then opened them.

"Oh, Inma?"

She growled softly.

"Is it true that Randi and Arvid are thinking of going back to Norway?"

By way of reply she pulled a pillow over her head, so I chose not to pursue the subject.

8

"Is it true that Randi and Arvid are thinking of going back to Norway?" I asked her after I'd begun my breakfast quietly, as she doesn't like to be babbled at first thing in the morning.

She frowned at her cornflakes. "She hasn't said so. She's only told me that they're getting on quite well and that Arvid has cut down slightly on his cycling. Toast?"

"But has she not hint—"

"*Toast?*"

"Yes, please. Very well, not another word about them, oh great hater of gossip."

Over coffee I told her that after swiftly showing the Belgians their turbine options I meant to visit more chalets down in that windswept wilderness. "But I'll be back by lunchtime, to see what you've painted."

"I'll paint a little this afternoon. I'm coming with you this morning."

"Are you?"

She smiled. Yes, I'm curious to see how you operate. It'll only be this once, and who knows, I may be able to make some suggestions."

"All right," I said, sure that she wanted to check out my Belgian buddies. I felt like calling Lars and asking him to hide a few sinks and bidets and maybe shove the organ out of sight, but there was no escaping the fact that Inma was going to see their place in all its cluttered splendour. I feared she would view them as half-mad hoarders and frown upon my future visits, because Inma lacks the bohemian streak which I cunningly hide beneath my conformist facade, or so I told myself at the time.

As luck would have it, Inma's phone soon pinged, heralding a text message from her darling daughter. She frowned, then smiled, then frowned again.

"What does she say?"

"Not a lot. 'Please pick me up at Elda station on Friday afternoon. Staying till Tuesday. Looking forward to working with the old man. Hugs, Natalia.' Oh, that's just like her to give so little notice! Damn it, I'll have to clean the whole annex today."

I sighed, stood up, and softly grasped my keys. "I won't be too long then. Look, why don't you paint this morning, then we'll both clean this afternoon?"

"I can't paint this morning."

"Why not?"

"Because I'm coming with you." A smile flickered on her lovely lips. "Hmm, her mission with Zefe is what has made her come, so maybe she should stay with them, to be closer to her subject."

I remembered shifting the junk from Álvaro's second bedroom into the third when Zefe had been about to move in. "Er, I don't think that'll be feasible, unless she wants to camp at the foot of his bed." I recalled how frisky he'd been in hospital. "Though I wouldn't advise it. No, it'll have to be here or the annex. Is she coming alone?"

She sent a quick text and Natalia soon answered in the affirmative.

"I'll just prepare a room for her then. Come on, let's go."

She became positively chirpy in the car, as at Christmas in Murcia she'd barely had twenty minutes alone with her daughter, but a worried expression soon suffused my own face. She noticed this.

"Oh, Alan, I don't really mind what the Belgians are like, you know. I'm not as averse to unusual people as you sometimes think."

"It isn't that. I'm thinking about Natalia's mission. I believe Zefe's been behaving well and they've established a status quo of unprecedented harmony. Álvaro's words, not mine."

"Oh, well, if Natalia's a little disappointed it won't matter. She'll be able to spend more time with us." She frowned. "Oh, I see, that's why you're looking so glum."

I denied this vile aspersion. "In fact I hope she sees immediately that her brilliance is no longer required in their household and spends the rest of her time by our side."

"You mean you fear that she may upset their state of harmony?"

"I certainly do. Zefe's mind is always on a knife's edge between conformity and rebellion. She may tweak the knife and all hell might break loose."

"I'll speak to her before she meets them."

As I was driving along the road not far from her bar she remembered to tell me that they'd given a few of my leaflets to customers.

"Don't waste them, dear. I'll receive another packet soon, but it's hard work writing my name and number on them all."

"Sheer hell, yes, I remember doing it. That's why we taped one to the bar, so anyone who's interested has to ask for one."

I patted her leg. "You think of everything, love."

Inma got on well with Nina and Lars, possibly because their bourgeois background was only thinly disguised by their nonconformist lifestyle. Lars, soon sporting his false tooth and a better pair of glasses, became very businesslike as I described the features of the four feasible wind turbines in my catalogue, but soon expressed dissatisfaction with the size of the largest one.

"The diameter's 1.78 metres," I said.

"Yes, far too small. 2000W even on very windy days won't be nearly enough."

"I suppose I can ask my boss if we could get bigger ones."

Once again he checked that my coffee cup was empty. "Let's go to the site."

After we'd all trooped up to the ridge he began to pace around, licking and raising his finger several times, before placing three stones on the weedy ground, about five metres apart.

"Hmm, yes, about there, but on a windier day I'll make a final decision."

"Oh, so do you want three then?"

"Yes, we'll see how we go with three."

"Rather than one big one?"

"Yes. I'm no expert, but I believe that in gentle winds three small ones will produce some energy, while a larger one may fail to rotate at all."

"Hmm, that makes sense."

"Come on, let's decide how many batteries we'll need."

Back at the house Nina took Inma to see her paintings, a fortuitous move for me, because when I suggested just a couple of batteries for backup Lars referred to the small print in the catalogue which indicated that this type of turbine wasn't designed to be connected to the network.

"Ah, yes, I must have missed that bit. Gracias, Lars."

"So we'll have six for now. Yes, and once the turbines are up and running we'll look into the panels."

"Panels too?"

He smiled. "Alan, like most supposedly alternative folk we wish to be independent of the powers that be. Your timely arrival has made us reflect on our tardiness in embracing renewable energy, so naturally we'll wish to go off-grid eventually. Let's see how your company installs the turbines first though, as I loathe shoddy workmanship."

I wondered if his denture plugged directly into his brain and turned this zany photographer into a hard-boiled operator. I wondered about something else too.

"When did you learn to speak Castilian so well, Lars?"

"During the five years we spent in Buenos Aires. We speak fluent German, English and Italian too, plus a few other languages less proficiently."

"And French and Flemish, of course."

"Yes."

"So is it the Walloons who speak mainly French in Belgium?"

"Yes, plus Walloon and sometimes the Picard dialect, but don't you think we should concluded our business before we discuss other things, Alan?"

"Ah, right, yes."

He soon called Nina in to approve the order for just under €5000 worth of gear, before signing it, ruffling his frizzy hair, and unclipping his denture, which he popped into his shirt pocket. He grinned at Inma. "And now for a little photography."

About an hour later we were back on the road. After such a profitable outing I suggested calling it a day and dropping in on Cathy and Bernie.

She tutted. "Oh, no, you still have work to do." She slid out the uncut photo from her very own jigsaw puzzle. "The effect that her camerawork has produced is really quite remarkable."

"Yes, it's surprising what they can do with an old birdcage, a big teddy bear and a beautiful woman like you. I'll show you mine when we get home. Do you like Nina and Lars then?"

"Of course, they're very likeable people."

I rubbed my hands up and down each side of the steering wheel. "I'll buy a camera tomorrow."

"Very likeable people who do interesting things, but you must go your own way, Alan."

"Of course." I grinned. "I mean to invent my very own way of doing... whatever it is I'm going to do."

"I'm not sure I like the sound of that. Turn into this little hamlet."

"Bah, it's just a few decrepit houses. The old peasants in them wouldn't know a solar panel if it slapped them in the face. I give dumps like that a wide berth, as I'd only get chased by a savage dog or a psychopathic goat."

"Nevertheless we ought to take a look."

"Muy bien."

A mean-looking mutt did indeed greet us as we stepped out of the car, but as it was only about nine inches tall I manfully shooed it away, though it lingered to see what we were up to. Of the ten or so houses on either side of the unpaved street, several had their window shutters closed, but I had to admit that many of the shutters were in surprisingly good nick.

"Of course they are. I guess these are mostly second homes now, although that one appears to be occupied."

I peered at a square of hand-painted tiles next to the sturdy new door. "Oh, God, look at that."

"Hmm, Rose Cottage. That's a nice name."

"These damned guiris get everywhere," I grumbled, before looking up at the recently re-tiled roof. "No panels though. They probably find them aesthetically unpleasing. I'm surprised they haven't thatched the bloody roof."

Inma chuckled. "Why has such a simple house name turned you against these potential customers?"

I began to explain the twee connotations which Rose Cottage had for me, before focussing on the final part of her statement. "...but, as you say, they are potential customers. Ah!" I closed my eyes and turned around.

"What on earth are you doing now?"

"Trying to guess how one is meant to hail them, and I promise I haven't noticed. I believe you'll find, in the centre of the door, a heavy and highly polished... thing, made of brass, which one has to lift and bang down."

"That's right, now–"

"Ha! I knew it. Right, now I'm going to guess its shape. If it isn't a rose, which wouldn't surprise me, I bet it's an animal. Yes, a... a hedgehog, or a rabbit. Am I right?"

"No, it's a plain one. The word is aldaba and one can buy them in the shops. Now open your eyes and stop fooling around. I'm beginning to regret having come with you."

"Sorry." I began to move on, but she grabbed my arm, gave the knocker three sharp raps, and thrust me into the doorway.

"I'm not in the right frame of mind now," I whimpered.

"It serves you right. Goodness me, what a clown!"

Fortunately the occupants of Rose Cottage weren't at home, so I whipped out a leaflet, which Inma intercepted before it reached the brass letterbox.

I shrugged. "OK, suits me. Does your infallible instinct tell you they won't buy panels then?"

"No, you cretin (sic). Go for the personal touch. Write a little note on one, so they'll be sure you're British."

I fluttered the leaflet. "Alas, my name and number fill all the little boxes."

She stomped back to the car and returned flourishing a pad of post-its.

"Ah, you think of everything, dear."

"And you think of nothing." She smacked the pad into my hand, followed by a pen, then dictated the simple message I was to write in English, so I got to work.

"...all the best, Alan. Should I add a couple of kisses?" I quipped, but she'd marched off along the street, so me and the little mongrel meekly followed. I noticed that its tail was curled between its legs.

"I know how you feel," I said in English. "We'd better try to buck up our ideas."

Outside the last rather shabby house I found Inma chatting to an elderly lady.

"She's wasting her time here," I murmured to my companion, but of course she wasn't, because after passing the time of day she asked the stout matron about the neighbours. It turned out that all the houses except Rose Cottage had Spanish owners, mostly locals who now lived in nearby towns.

"But some of them come most weekends," She smiled. "It's more lively here then, and even more so in summer."

After making a little more small talk, Inma then explained that *she* represented a solar energy company. "So I'm going to leave a leaflet at each house. Here's yours."

"Oh, I shouldn't think we'll bother with that sort of thing."

Inma beamed. "Well, just in case you do. It's been lovely to meet you."

The lady's false teeth gleamed in the sun. "You too, dear."

"What are the British people like?" I asked rather abruptly.

"What British people?"

I pointed. "The ones in the house with the foreign name."

"Oh, they're from Ireland. We all know now that we oughtn't to call them ingleses, but they're ever so nice and always ready to lend a hand. I'm glad they came, because now we have company all the time."

We said goodbye and Inma led the way to the next house. I noticed that the mutt's tail was now wagging, but my figurative one certainly was not.

"What is the meaning of this, Inma?"

"Of what?"

"Since when do *you* represent a solar energy company?"

"Since it became expedient. I shall write notes to these people and the lady will speak well of me. If anyone calls you, you're to say we work together, then I'll come to try to make a sale, as you would undoubtedly mess things up."

I shook my head. "Harsh words."

"But true ones. Oh, the opportunities you'd waste without me don't bear thinking about! What's the point of having a Five Year Plan if by the end of it we won't be able to afford anything better than a crummy apartment in some dreadful seaside place?"

I pictured Joseph Stalin and thought him a relatively benign figure compared to Inma in one of these moods. "Not a Five Year Plan, but a New Deal, but this is ridiculous. You have your own work, and plenty of it."

"I know, but I've just had a remarkable idea."

I glanced at the mutt and saw its tail sticking up and one front paw raised. "What is it?"

"You'll find out soon enough. I'll write the notes and you stick them to the leaflets and deliver them." She wrote the first one and pointed at a door. "You'll be able to manage that, won't you?"

I growled at her, the mutt growled at me, then I did her bidding, before insisting that she occupy the driver's seat in the car too. On the way back she pointed out three more hamlets where *we* ought to try a similar tactic.

"We could call at the weekend, of course, but I think with this sort of product and with such a lot of ground to cover it's better to distribute leaflets with a nice little note in the hamlets and villages, preferably after meeting someone and making a good impression," she chirped. "You can go on visiting chalets alone, but you must leave a note with the leaflet if they aren't in. Ah, and I'll write a few notes too, so if you believe the owners are Spanish you can leave one of mine." She chuckled. "I do believe that together we can make a success of this, Alan."

Benumbed by her now gleeful state, I quietly pointed out that I, Alan Laycock, had been recruited to flog the solar gear, not her.

"Oh, you can still take the orders. I don't want the glory, just the income."

"Let's go to my sister's," I said, feeling in need of some moral support which they may or may not give me, but at least Inma would have to rationalise her peculiar proposition in the presence of witnesses.

When she emitted something akin to a cackle I stiffened. Was she losing her marbles? Had my erratic ways finally driven her over the edge? Would the men in white coats have to be summoned due to two and half years of unwitting mental abuse having finally washed her up on the shores of cloud cuckoo land?

"Are you feeling all right, love?" I purred.

"I've never felt better. We're going to the bar."

"All right," I said, sure that Rosa would make her see sense.

After a short consultation with Rosa in the kitchen, the pair of them emerged wearing worryingly mischievous expressions.

"Should we explain the plan, or just spring it upon him?" Inma said to her partner.

"There's no time like the present."

"Then I'll go to my sister-in-law's and we'll come along later."

"All right."

"Hasta luego, Alan," said Inma.

"Come here, you," said Rosa. "And you too, Jorge."

The dozy waiter and I arrived at the bar and Rosa opened the hatch.

"Jorge, you're now going to teach Alan everything you know."

"Me?" said he.

"Eh?" said I.

"Step this way," said she, before closing the hatch and joining Randi in the kitchen.

"Hola, Alan. What's this about?"

My muddled mind spotted a ray of hope. "Er, you're to show me what you do, because I'll be covering your holiday."

"But that's not for over a month. You might forget. I know I would."

I sighed. "I've got a feeling I won't. Remind me of the prices, Jorge."

"Well, well, well," said Bernie at about four o'clock. "I hurried down, hoping to see you slaving away, and here you are in the corner, tucking into a tasty plate of paella."

I brandished my fork. "No time to eat till now," I mumbled with my mouth full. "I let Jorge eat first, as the lad was starving."

He patted me on the back, before taking a seat. "Jorge! A cortado over here, and don't forget to heat the milk," he yelled in Spanish.

"Hey, you remembered the subjunctive. No olvide*s*. Muy bien."

"Naturalmente. So, how are you enjoying your new job?"

"It's been fun, but is that what it is, a new job? Rosa won't tell me what Inma's idea is. She just orders me around, and I must say it makes a change from having to make decisions all the time. We had fifteen in for lunch and without me Jorge would have struggled, poor lad. He did show me how to make a proper carajillo though. You know, with a coffee bean and a bit of lemon and setting fire to the brandy."

"Jorge! Stop the cortado. I'll have a carajillo."

"OK, Bernie."

"Lucky he's so slow. Well, I thought you might be distraught, but you seem to have taken to it pretty well."

I shrugged and swallowed a mouthful of rice. "It's a long time since I worked for someone else, if you don't count the hotel."

"I don't. Yes, it's over ten years since your last proper job."

"So long?"

"Yep. I remember it was during the last economic crash when they fired you from that big bakery."

"I walked. It was too bloody hot around those nasty ovens. After that I just sold my coins. So what's Inma's had to say about all this?"

"Oh, that you're going to fill in for her when she thinks she might seal a deal that you'd mess up."

I nodded. "I thought so. Ha, she thinks that by sweet talking one old dear and then shoving her cute little notes through a few letterboxes that the orders are going to start pouring in." I shook my head. "She's so naive about sales." Bernie just sipped his carajillo. "Don't you think? I mean, you're the expert, after all."

"You already know what I think about Inma's ability as a saleswoman."

"Do I? Oh, you mean the price she got for the cave house."

"Yes, and the way she got it. She's a natural, whereas you're... well, you're..."

"Let me have it, Bern. Rosa doesn't mince her words, so neither should you."

"You could never hold down a sales job, because you'd be too inconsistent. You have to adapt to every kind of punter, you see. You have to know when to joke around and when to be serious, when to put on the pressure and when to go for the soft sell." He shrugged. "Your scope is limited, which isn't to say that you won't make the odd really good sale that even I might have fluffed. Inma's been telling us about your plans to retire to the seaside."

"Yes, that's another recent brainwave of hers. What do you think of that?"

He moved his head from side to side in the Spanish way. "Not much at first. Renting goes against the grain for us Brits. Throwing money away, we think, but I suppose if you get a good deal and manage to save a lot, it'll work out fine. It was a bit of a surprise though, I must say."

"For me too, but she loves the sea. I guess renting will keep our options open. Who knows, we might decide to retire to the northern coast. Do you not fancy the seaside for your old age, Bern?"

He shuddered, then held up his calloused hands. "What'd I do with these down there, build sandcastles? No, us farmers are wedded to the land, *our* land."

"I thought you might say that."

"You know, some of my old mates have told me that their dads, or maybe their granddads, never saw the sea, or only once or twice in their lives. And why would they? Though it's only thirty miles away it was like another... planet for those hardy men, whose horizons only stretched to... to the horizon, if that."

I stifled a yawn. "Yes, Bernie."

"Though I suppose you could say the same for us lot in Lancashire. Until the trains came I bet hardly anyone from our neck of the woods went to Blackpool. Then the Wakes Weeks began and we started to get a taste for the exotic." He shrugged, then stamped his foot. "We need to learn to stay put again and keep our feet on the ground."

I smiled. "You only narrowly escaped a visit home last summer."

He gritted his teeth, then smiled. "Yeah, it was lucky your Aunt Maud finally snuffed it, may she rest in peace. Even Cathy can hardly force me to go to see my own sister if I don't want to. Nope, I don't plan on leaving this brown and pleasant land again, touch wood."

"I do. I feel I still have plenty of travelling to do. Did Inma mention the Belgians?"

"Briefly. Sound like a pair of nuts to me. I mean, filling their land with junk instead of cultivating it... como Dios manda (as God commands)."

"Horses for courses, Bern. Each of us must find his own way."

"Garçon!" Cathy cried from the doorway. "We want coffee."

"Oh, let the poor boy eat," Inma said in English. "He must be exhausted."

Rosa emerged from the kitchen, followed by a radiant Randi, and the four ladies were soon clustered around our table, watching me eat and discussing my waitering debut.

"Was he awfully slow?" Inma asked Rosa.

"Well, compared to our... our friend there behind the bar, he didn't seem too bad, but then who would? He needs to learn how to carry plates without sticking his thumbs in the food though."

"I'll make him practise at home."

"Is he polite to the customers?" Cathy asked, the past tense still being a scarcely opened book to her, despite her fabulous vocabulary.

Rosa nodded. "Yes, almost too obsequious really. I believe he was born to serve."

"And he came to help me when I was really busy," said Randi, earning me a frown from Inma, who may not have approved of me rubbing elbows with the curvaceous and still flirtatious blonde in the confines of the kitchen.

"Then he took the plates to the wrong table, but apologised so profusely that they all laughed," said Rosa.

I pushed away my empty plate and stiffened my spine. "I merely adapted to circumstances." Up went my chin. "There's a time to be masterful and a time to know one's place."

They were all having a good laugh about this when old Juan Antonio approached.

"You're six minutes late," said Bernie, tapping his watch.

"No, I've been talking to Jorge. So, Alan, have your enterprises failed and now you're reduced to this?"

"No, and why *reduced* to this?"

He shrugged. "A man who works for his wife is a... an unfortunate man."

"Go away, you old sexist," said Inma, giving him a friendly shove.

"Poor Alan," he murmured as he retired to his table.

I stood up. "Now, if you don't mind, I have work to do."

"Sit down and have a coffee," said Rosa. "I think Jorge can handle four customers."

I remained standing. "All right, but first I'll take your order. Please be seated, ladies."

I then indulged in a little buffoonery, first assisting them into their chairs, then leaning over them with my little pad and a cheesy smile, a bit like Basil Fawlty. After bowing and scraping in a most amusing manner, I handed the pad to Manuel, I mean Jorge, and sat down.

"Has no-one been rude to him?" Inma asked Rosa.

"No."

"Pity. Only when some oaf berates him will we see if he can handle it, or if he reacts like the character he was just imitating," she said, having watched our Fawlty Towers DVDs more than once.

"I'm more resilient than you think, cariño." Having had a cunning thought, I turned to Rosa. "Now, jefa (boss), as the sweet Natalia is coming this weekend, her mother will wish to spend lots of time with her, but I'll be more than happy to come here and cover for her."

Rosa looked at Inma, who looked at me. "That will depend on how busy Natalia is with your old friends, Alan."

I groaned, having forgotten about the imminent Natalia-Zefe encounter. "Not very busy, I expect," I muttered.

Inma finished her coffee and stood up. "You can go and lay the groundwork for their meeting now."

"Oh, will my trials never end!"

"Go back to the land, my son, and forget about the complications of the modern world," said Bernie.

"We're going into town to buy a new dishwasher," said Cathy.

"Oh, woe are us, eh, mate?"

"Yes, indeed."

Inma dropped me off at the end of Álvaro's street and half an hour later I was able to tell her that all was peace and love in their household.

"Did you mention that Natalia would be visiting them?"

"I told Álvaro. He asked me why and I said I didn't know exactly, but that I thought she wished to do some kind of research."

"How did he take that?"

"Worriedly."

She frowned. "I'll give her strict instructions not to annoy Zefe."

"Yes, or provoke him, or overexcite him. Oh, it'll be all right." I perched on the arm of the sofa and stroked her hair. "Now, dear breadwinner," I said in English. "How much am I allowed to spend on a camera tomorrow?"

She told me.

"Aw, is that all?"

"It's quite enough for something that will end up in the back of a drawer."

"Ha, we'll see about that."

Although I wasn't in the mood, I went to tinkle the ivories of my keyboard, having just remembered how much it had cost.

9

Armed with my nifty Sony compact camera which had left me with zero change from the measly €200 that I'd been allowed to spend, I paid Juanca a visit. The previous evening Inma had instructed me to call Liz and Ben to tell them that the house sale could proceed forthwith, for which they seemed exceedingly grateful, them being fed up to the back teeth of the Bigastro expat scene by then.

"So we're now looking for a house to rent," I told Juanca after relating our new plan of action.

"To rent is to throw money away, Alan. You British seem to know that better than anyone."

"Flexibility is our motto now, my friend. Cheap rent and a healthy income is the key to our comfortable retirement, five to ten years from now."

"No, Alan, house prices are rising, so you must buy now and sell later. What else can you do with the money from the cave house, now that the banks are giving hardly any interest?"

I smiled. "Buy and sell coins. I'm going to get back into that, as well as selling lots of panels, with Inma's help."

"Eh?"

I outlined our new partnership.

He scratched his head. "So you'll work at the bar when she feels she has more chance of selling. Hmm, I see, I think."

"Yes, it was a joint decision, of course, but one that we feel will increase our income."

"I don't doubt it."

I chose that moment to whip out my new camera and snap a shot of his ugly mug.

"What's that piece of rubbish?"

I viewed the screen. "You blinked."

He patted his hair. "Take another one if you must."

"No, this is the kind of thing I'm after. I'm going to do sort of artistic stuff, you see, though I don't know quite what yet."

He sighed. "Oh, you should have asked me about cameras, Alan."

"Why? Are you an expert?"

He smiled sadly. "I'm an expert at spending money, as I confessed to you during our delightful walk."

"Ah, another spending spree?"

"I'm afraid so, in Barcelona that time. I bought... but I won't bore you with the details. I spent over €7,000 on three cameras, each more expensive than the last. I've used only one of them, once, and now regret my purchases from the bottom of my heart. Digital cameras depreciate quickly, you see, and if there's one thing I hate it's a reduction of my assets. If you were to buy one of them, you'd be doing me a great favour."

"Too late, I'm afraid. I've just blown my whole budget on this little beauty."

He scowled. "Take that silly toy back to the shop and relieve me of my compact Fujifilm. It cost me a thousand but you can have it for si… seven hundred."

"Hmm, and what will it do that this one won't?"

After rambling on about sensors and lens quality for a while, he clicked his fingers. "Oh, I forgot to tell you about something far more important. An English couple came yesterday, wishing to sell their house."

"A tetchy old man and his agreeable wife?"

"That's right, and they mentioned your name."

I shrugged nonchalantly, having prepared myself for this pivotal moment in my house-selling career, though I decided to hear him out first, for old times' sake.

"Anyway, I went to see the house out on that windswept plain where no-one in their right mind would choose to live. I have two potential buyers, both Danish, funnily enough, but I suppose their little country is so cramped that their desire for open spaces outweighs their common sense. Anyway, as is my custom, I asked them how much they wanted for the place and I feel sure that one of the Danish couples will cough up enough to make it a worthwhile enterprise for the two of us."

From the moderate fiendishness of his subsequent cackle I estimated that he planned to hike up the price by ten or fifteen thousand, something he was able to do by means of a judicious inclusion of a cash amount, followed by a cunning game of non-musical chairs at the notary's office, as I'd seen for myself once upon a time.

After rising to my full height of four foot six (seated) I cleared my throat. "No, gracias, Juanca."

He sighed. "Oh, please don't subject me to yet another bout of moral gymnastics, before finally accepting the cash, as always."

"There'll be none of that. I don't want a cent, not from this couple or any... well, I'm not saying that I'll never, ever accept a commission from you again, but not this time."

He glanced at his watch and looked through the dusty window. "Let me know when you've talked yourself into it, Alan."

"No, my decision is final, in this particular case, so try to be a little less greedy this time."

He shrugged. "I won't make all that much, but as you wish."

Relieved that I'd stuck to my guns – or rather our guns, as Inma had also frowned upon me making a tidy sum from the elderly couple – I asked him if he could help us to find a house to rent. "Ideally from the beginning of March, when the house sale ought to have gone through."

He stretched his arms, rearranged the crotch area of his pleated trousers, and yawned. "Oh, what a bore! I don't usually bother with rentals, as the rewards are so paltry, but I'll make a few enquiries, if you're sure you wish to commit this blunder."

"We are, and it isn't a blunder, it's a... mere pause on our way up the housing ladder."

"Translating from English again, I see, but I've heard this housing ladder mentioned before by your compatriots. What does it mean exactly?"

I explained.

He shook his head. "How unutterably stupid. Under normal circumstances one should move house no more than twice in one's life. Just think of the fuss and the costs involved each time, but I guess I shouldn't complain. Ha, some British come to the coast, then move inland, then back to the coast, and many end up back in Britain, often to some unknown place which has taken their fancy. What's wrong with you? Do you not value your roots? Why not just come here in the summer months, instead of leaving your lives behind like a…. a discarded camera?"

I chuckled. "I didn't know you felt so strongly about it."

"Bah, I couldn't care less. It's their loss." He stood up and began to pace around. "Now, speaking of cameras, before my spending spree I did study the subject in some depth, and I can't bear to see a friend of mine using such a pitiful device. Take it back to the shop and I'll bring you the Fujifilm tomorrow."

"I can't afford it."

"It will be a gift."

"Oh, graci… hang on, what's the catch?"

No catch. It's simply a token of my appreciation for your assistance in the past and the future."

"But not the present, eh? If it's meant to be an indirect payment for sending that couple to you, I'm afraid I can't accept it."

"Not at all. Forget them. It's a gesture of goodwill, nothing more, and will rid me of one small source of annoyance."

I smiled. "You could give me all three cameras, then your spending spree will soon be forgotten."

"You jest, I hope, but if you give me further cause to feel grateful to you, I may reward you with my Canon mirrorless, or even my valuable Nikon, although my gratitude will have to be great to make me part with that marvellous machine."

My better side almost caused me to protest against these tempting enticements to find him more customers, but rather than split hairs I thanked him for his imminent gift and trotted off to the electronics shop to return the Sony. The lady accepted it fairly graciously, as we'd bought several items there, rather than inspecting the goods then buying them online as she claimed many people were wont to do. After collecting a fat envelope full of leaflets from the post office, I headed off to make a few swift sales before lunch, armed also with two post-it pads full of ingratiating notes which Inma and I had written the previous evening, at her instigation, of course.

At the first chalet I approached I saw a car with a *Bebé a Bordo* sticker in the rear window, so, assuming them to be Spaniards, I swiftly stuck one of Inma's post-its onto a leaflet and thrust it into the letterbox, as it wouldn't do to encroach on her territory and risk fluffing a sale. At the next chalet the Spanish-registered car sported a GB sticker and I was about to rattle the gate, there being no bell, when I remembered Inma saying that with the leaflets we'd cover more ground, so I slapped one of my post-its onto one and was soon trundling merrily towards a tiny hamlet. There the resident mutt was at least ten inches tall, but from its forlorn expression and the presence of only three dusty cars I concluded that it was another cluster of second homes, so after pre-attaching Inma's post-its I whizzed from door to door with the leaflets. On driving off I glanced in the mirror and saw a man hailing me through the dust that I'd raised, but I'd begun to enjoy the speediness of my progress so much that I just wound down my window and gave him a thumbs-up sign.

By then I'd convinced myself that this blitzkrieg leafleting method would be far more effective than wasting time chewing the fat with folk who would be unlikely to buy, so by the time I arrived home at six, having stopped off for a bite to eat in a distant bar, I'd covered over fifty kilometres and distributed an awful lot of leaflets. I feared that Inma wouldn't wholly approve of this total omission of visits, but fortunately she didn't know how fat the envelope had been. Unfortunately she did know how fat her post-its pad had been, so I set about writing more notes in a feminine hand, not for her perusal, of course, but in order not to run out of hers anytime soon. I felt a little guilty about this slight dereliction of duty, however, and vowed to mend my ways after Natalia's visit, as in a stress-free state I'd feel more inclined to come face to face with our prospective customers.

"Stop kidding yourself," I said into the bathroom mirror a while later. "If you're not careful your fear of rejection, and rabid dogs, will turn you into a mere leaflet courier, and before you know it you'll have covered your whole area."

"So what?" I replied. "Then I'll start again, having given them time to assimilate the idea of solar power, and make sales left, right and centre."

"Wishful thinking, mate."

"Yeah, I guess it is."

"Alan? Who's there?"

I scurried out. "Oh, just singing, tra-la-la." I grinned. "Mocina, dame un besin, pa guardalu hasta que vuelva-ah-a..." I trilled. "Do you remember that one, love?"

She looked me up and down and frowned. "I believe you've done something you're ashamed of. Don't tell me you've spent a lot of money on a camera."

"Not a cent, my love. Juanca's going to give me a little one he never uses."

"Why?"

"Out of the goodness of his heart."

"He hasn't got one. Tell me the truth."

So I summarised our little chat, even admitting that the camera was new and costly.

"I see. Well, the next time you go to the Belgians' you ought to also visit that British couple, to thank them for the camera which they've indirectly gifted you."

"Oh, now you're looking for the cat's fifth leg," I said, which means to split hairs.

She shrugged. "Well, at least you didn't accept any money this time, or did you?"

I clasped my heart. "May lightning strike me if I did."

"All right."

I switched on the kettle, relieved to have deflected her attention from my more serious shortcomings, but not for long, as she soon asked me if I'd paid many visits.

I reached into a cupboard for a fresh box of teabags. "Yes, er... quite a few."

She moved closer. "Where did you get to?"

I stooped to retrieve the box which had slid through my hands. "Oh, you know, here and there."

"Where?"

I fumbled with the slippery PG Tips box. "Oh, south, then east a bit, then north. Sort of a circle, you know." I arose to find her arms crossed and her face crosser, and short of ducking into a drawer I could evade her gaze no longer.

"Alan?"

"Sí?"

"I heard what you said in the bathroom, or some of it, as I've no idea how long your dialogue had been going on."

I cursed myself for having recently oiled the front door hinges, a rare venture into the field of home maintenance for me.

"Ah, well, in that case, what can I say?"

"You know, you often lie after seeing Juanca. It must be contagious. Maybe you should avoid him from now on."

"Yes, I will, after I've got my camera."

She couldn't help but laugh.

"And he's going to keep his eyes open for houses to rent, for us, for no charge."

"Hmm."

"And tomorrow morning I promise to make a few proper visits."

"No, go on as you are. As you were saying to yourself just now, it's better to let them have a think about it first."

"Yes."

"Before *I* go and pay some visits."

"Yes."

"While you work in the bar."

"Yes."

"A nice change for both of us."

"Yes, I like working there. I have to do what I have to do and I can't take the shortcuts which I occasionally, er... avail myself of."

"Yes, and Rosa was quite pleased with you."

"Really?"

"Yes, and she thinks you'll be good for business."

"Really? Why, because I'm so handsome, ha ha?"

"Not exactly, but your bearing does have something to do with it."

I rose to my full height of six foot one, and some, due to a radical tilt of the chin.

"And especially the fact that you're a foreigner. For some reason people still have a sort of grudging respect for all things foreign, including gangly men who speak Castilian well, so she thinks you may add a certain *je ne sais quoi* to our outfit, goodness knows why."

I struck a statuesque pose. "Well, my dear, I–"

"No, Alan, none of your nonsense now, please. You've been a naughty boy today and I shouldn't be telling you this, but Rosa thinks you'll be an asset and that suits me fine, because I'd rather be selling panels than doing the same old thing."

She allowed me to enfold her in my arms. "Ah, what a well-matched couple we are, Inma! The combination of your strengths and my weaknesses will make us a force to be reckoned with, and now, my dear, I'll prepare your supper." I made for the microwave.

Later when the silent Charlie Chaplin film we'd been watching ended, Inma declared me to be the most peculiar person she'd ever known.

"Ah, what a master of comedy Chaplin was... peculiar, eh?"

"Yes, ever since I broke the news that you're going to be spending far more time at the bar than either of us expected, you've been laughing and joking like a little child, even before the film began."

"And what's wrong with that?"

"Most men when demoted to menial duties would be devastated, their pride shattered into tiny fragments, but you... you seem positively pleased about it."

"And so I am. The thing is, you didn't know me before. I spent fifty years shirking responsibility, so in a way I'm returning to my natural state. I believe I'm not intrinsically lazy, or no more than the next man, and working at the bar's going to be such a lark, being bossed around by Rosa and never having to make a single decision. Ah, yes, and besides that I'm going to pop a leaflet into every eligible letterbox for miles around. Drive, insert, drive, insert, stop for a coffee, drive, insert. Oh, what a carefree life it's going to be!

Inma grawned. (A combined groan and yawn.)

I slapped the sofa cushion. "And then, when my happy-go-lucky daytime chores are over, I'll return here to employ my enviable intellect to good effect."

"By setting the microwave?"

"Ha, very good. No, by selecting a few choice coins to bid on, thus reminding myself that as well as a waiter-cum-courier, I'm also a numismatic power to be reckoned with. Oh, yes, I'm going to have a lovely time."

"Don't forget to pick up Natalia at four tomorrow."

I spun around, laid my head on her lap, and smiled up at her. "Inma, I'll be delighted to. Nothing can possibly impair my excellent new outlook on life, not even Zefe's reaction to whatever she has up her sleeve."

"My thoughts entirely. Whatever goes on in that house will be no concern of mine."

"Nor mine. Oh, have you ever mentioned Zefe's tall tales to her?"

"I don't believe I've mentioned him at all."

I rubbed my hands together, then stroked her cheeks. "Even better."

10

On Friday I accomplished a satisfactory morning's work without so much as starting the car. Fran called to tell me that the company would be installing Jesús's panels on Monday without fail, so I rang the Chippenham couple and promised to accompany them there on Wednesday, just in case they failed. No sooner had I put down my phone than a chalet owner called to express interest in our products. Due to the vast expanse of almost luminous gravel in his compound I'd stuck one of my post-its on the leaflet, but the man was of native stock, so after consulting Inma I called back to tell him that my number-one saleswoman would soon be paying him a visit. I then called Fran again to confess that my wife would be giving me a hand now and then.

"I'm glad about that, Alan. She seems like a dynamic lady and I believe she'll be successful with the Spanish customers."

"That's what I thought. Bye, Fran."

A short time later Juanca phoned to tell me that the camera awaited me in his office, so, fatigued by so many calls, I made a cup of tea and read up on the Fujifilm X100T, a fixed lens camera with a leaf shutter which produced pictures of astonishing quality, according to the reviews. After pondering on what kind of artistic images I intended to take on the handsome device, I sought inspiration on the internet and stumbled upon an idea that I thought might be just the thing for me, as it required little apparent skill, ought to keep me clicking merrily away for some time to come, and might eventually impress Lars and Nina.

Refreshed by my constructive hour of downtime, I began to peruse eBay in search of a few coin bargains. One way to do this – and it applies to all types of things – is to insert a suitable search term, click the 'Newly Listed' box, and keep refreshing the page, because with patience one may find an underpriced 'buy it now' offer, or a recently commenced low-starting-price auction for a lovely item which might well achieve a higher price than the seller anticipates. The trick here is to make them an appetising offer, then to allay their suspicions that they might have a real winner on their hands by claiming that you need the coin/book/bike/camera etc. asap, because you're moving house, leaving the country or retiring to a monastery.

Responses I've received to this little ruse include, 'Piss off, you thief', 'Pull the other one, dude' and, more commonly, 'Thanks, but the auction will run its course', but every now and then they accept the offer and you congratulate yourself on your cunning. For this latter method to succeed, however, one normally has to spend many hours at the computer, but as I'd become such a busy man I just followed a few promising auctions and swore not to forget about them as I'd invariably done in recent times.

Feeling that I'd accomplished quite enough for one day, I then trundled into town and was soon fondling my sleek new snapper.

"Muchísimas gracias, Juanca. I really appreciate this gift."

"De nada."

"And as I'll be taking it everywhere, in order to carry out my new artistic project, you'll be in my thoughts constantly, so whenever I spot anything that may interest you I'll call you right away."

"Gracias, Alan. What's this artistic project?"

By way of reply I applied the viewfinder to my eye and approached him, before taking a close-up of his nose.

He tutted. "You'll have to use the macro mode to do that, or it'll come out blurred."

I viewed the image and frowned like Picasso after inserting a crucial squiggle. "No, this is just the right aesthetic effect I'm after."

He rubbed his nose. "Right, so what's the project?"

I smiled like Leonardo may have done after deciding to sketch a rough outline of a biggish supper party on a convent wall in Milan. "I'd rather not say just yet. The project is still in its... embryonic stage, but I'll let you know in due course." I snapped a passing lady with a pram. "And of course I'll invite you to the unveiling." I took a shot of the corner of his desk and perused it. "Hmm, pleasingly angular. Well, thanks again, Juanca, and I'll be in touch." I raised the camera to chest height, then took a lighter from his desk, lit it, and moved it towards his precious file.

"Hey! Noooo!"

Click. "Hmm, yes, the angst of the modern man. I'll use that. Hasta luego."

"Idiota!"

On my way back to the car I snapped away in a fairly random manner, usually at objects from close quarters, chuckling to myself all the while. My supposed project was but an idle whim which I thought might keep me amused until I found a more sensible use for my new toy, but I did nevertheless reinvest some of my camera money in a decent printer, as our old thing was past its best. The lady in the shop seemed pleased by my swift return visit, but less so when I photographed a big silver fridge.

"What's up, María José?"

"Folk do that on their phones, then buy elsewhere."

"Ha, not I! I'm commencing a photographic project, you see, thus the new printer."

"Then you'll need more ink, as there's hardly any in the cartridges that come with it."

So I spent the rest of my camera money, photographed her hand holding my receipt, and bade her a cheery good day.

When Natalia stepped down onto the platform at Elda train station just after four o'clock I immortalised the moment with a well-framed shot, before pocketing the camera and hurrying towards her with outstretched arms. I knew full well that she wasn't the hugging type, but I was determined to exude bonhomie during the entirety of her stay and not allow her to browbeat, bamboozle, annoy, anger, sadden or surprise me in any way.

She then surprised me by dropping her bag, hurtling into my arms, and squeezing most of the air from my chest.

"Oh, it's so good to see you, Alan!" she gushed after planting two proper kisses on my blushing cheeks, the pressure of her breasts having embarrassed me somewhat. When I'd got my breath back I noticed that her hair seemed glossier, her brown eyes shinier and her complexion healthier than just a few weeks earlier, when she'd mooched around her grandparents' flat for a few hours before shooting off to see her father in Alicante.

"And it's lovely to see you too... my dear."

She patted my cheek. "Oh, still the same stuffy old Alan, I see."

I grabbed her bag. "On the contrary, I'm a very carefree character nowadays."

"Me too."

"I'm glad about that. I mean, there's a time to be serious and a time to have fun, especially at your age."

"Well I'm having lots of fun right now."

"Ah, good."

"I've discovered the joys of sex, you see."

Oh, gawd, I thought. "Ah," I uttered.

"Come on, I'll tell you all about it on the way back."

She skipped along the platform while I trudged in her wake, steeling myself for the coming ordeal.

The good thing about driving was that I was able to squeeze the wheel or grasp the gearstick whenever her revelations became too much to bear. After telling me that Miguel, the drunken poet, had been a total flop and a terrible choice as a first lover, she moved onto her second boyfriend, a fellow student, who had been far too unadventurous.

"Partly because we always did it in bed."

Squeeze of the wheel. "Ah."

"Ha, as if there weren't lots more places to do it, like on a rug or in the kitchen," she said, her avid eyes beginning to bore a hole into my ruddy right cheek, or so it seemed. "And outside, of course, but it's been far too cold for that. I wanted to try in El Retiro last week, but Wilfredo wouldn't hear of it, him not being used to the freezing Madrid evenings. Anyway, Toni, my last lover, tried his best, but I think he simply lacked experience."

I changed down a gear, then up again, fearing that the conversation was about to take a more personal turn.

"And something else too. He was, well… but, no, I won't say it."

I nodded and began to prepare my next move.

"Because they say size isn't so important, but I'm not so sure about that now. What do you think, Alan?"

"I think we ought to talk about something else, Natalia. I don't know if you're trying to embarrass me on purpose, or if I find your natural frankness too… frank, but let's change the subject, por favor."

"Oh, you repressed old thing!"

"Merely reserved."

"How many lovers have you had?"

"Twenty-eight," I said without hesitation, before congratulating my brain on its rapid and, I believed, shrewd response. I'd upped the figure by twenty-odd, of course, but I felt that this impressive but not implausible number, coupled with the taciturnity I meant to maintain, ought to raise me in her estimation and possibly prevent further teasing.

"Liar."

I shrugged like Alfie, as played by Michael Caine.

"I'll ask Mamá."

Squeeze, gear change, mirror check, gear change, squeeze. "Er, I'd rather you didn't."

She tittered. "Why, have you lied to her?"

On suddenly remembering the existence of mobile phones, upon which explanatory texts can be quickly written, I smiled for the first time since leaving Elda. "Not at all. She knows the truth, but it's hardly kind to remind her of my, er... promiscuous past, is it?"

"Hmm, I'm still not sure if I believe you."

"It's unimportant anyway. Your mother's the only woman for me now."

"Wilfredo's slept with almost that number of women and he's only twenty-six."

"Bravo, he'll soon catch me up."

She huffed. "He will *not*."

"No, sorry. Where's he from?"

"The Dominican Republic."

"Ah."

"He's black."

"Nothing wrong with that."

"Who said there was?"

"The abruptness of your statement was meant to elicit a negative response, but I don't have a racist bone in my body."

"What?"

"Sorry, an English expression. What does Wilfredo do?"

She chuckled. "I'll tell you what he used to do. It explains why he's fu... slept with so many women. Can you guess?"

"Er, a basketball player? I believe sportsmen are very successful with the ladies."

She tutted. "That's a blatant racial stereotype, and he's a few centimetres shorter than you anyway."

"Ah."

"His height, I mean."

I coloured.

She patted my leg. "Don't worry, I'm not going to ask you anything so personal."

"I should think not."

"I'll ask Mamá."

I sighed, already composing the urgent text to this insufferable girl's mother.

"Wilfredo used to work as a sort of dance partner in Punto Cana, a resort in his country."

"I see."

"Though the dancing often led to more, as those American ladies were so sex-starved."

"Ah."

"But he only did that for a couple of summers when he was younger. Have a guess what he does now?"

"Er..." I warned myself to refrain from witty quips, as Natalia's sense of humour was as underdeveloped as her tactfulness. "Well, if he's in Madrid, I guess he must be doing some kind of job there."

"Like what? A waiter? A refuse operative? A car park attendant?"

"I don't have a class-conscious bone in my body, Natalia, and I don't give a damn what he does. I only hope that he's a good person and is the right man for you, assuming you think there's a future in your relationship, and that he treats you well even if he isn't," I semi-babbled.

"I can see Wilfredo and I going a long way together."

"Good."

"And do you know why?"

I groaned inwardly.

"I heard that. Wilfredo is about to complete his PhD. I met him in class; a class which he was teaching, about biological determinism regarding the African immigrants to the Greater Antilles."

"Uh-huh."

"Aren't you surprised?"

I shrugged. "Should I be?"

"Tonto!" she cried, before settling down to sulk, which suited me fine for a few miles, but on approaching the hamlet I admitted to being impressed by Wilfredo's achievements.

"I knew that," she said, throwing off her sulk like a silken sheet. "He hasn't had it easy, you know, as his parents are quite poor. He got a scholarship to study in Cuba and a government grant to come to Madrid to do his doctorate. He should complete that at about the same time as I finish my degree, so when I said we'd go far together I meant it. We'll find a really interesting project in some distant place and become the greatest anthropologist couple the world has ever known."

"I sincerely hope you do." I'd turned onto the track and soon spied Álvaro's house, but I decided not to mention the mission which had brought her here, hoping she might not begin to wreak havoc until the following day. As she appeared to have sex on the brain, I feared that my old pals wouldn't be spared her blunt observations and may even find themselves being given the third degree regarding their own sexual endeavours, as the impetuous little miss would be unlikely to respect their advanced age. This would embarrass Álvaro deeply and God alone knew how Zefe would react. In his countless tall tales he'd tended to eschew detailed accounts of his sexual conquests, merely intimating that he'd bedded at least one wench wherever he'd laid his hat, but were Natalia to question him directly he might get carried away, in more ways than one. I pictured her pinned against the wall in his iron grip and couldn't help smiling as the car rolled to a halt.

"And if you think I've forgotten about my main reason for coming, you're mistaken, Alan."

"Of course I haven't, but please remember that Zefe has been very ill and can't stand much excitement. Álvaro's heart is none too strong either, so I hope you'll comport yourself with tact and decorum."

"Of course I will. Whenever we anthropologists enter new terrain we must first put our subjects at their ease and avoid all confrontational comments. In this way we gain their confidence and elicit sincere responses to our enquiries."

"I'm glad to hear it. What, er… type of research do you have in mind?"

"Oh, I'm not sure. Mamá told me theirs was a conflictive cohabitation, so I may take a structural-functionalist approach, or possibly a more holistic one. We'll see."

"Hmm, I'd be holistic, if I were you. The thing is, the, er… conflictive cohabitation which your mother mentioned is no longer an issue, and we'd like to keep it that way."

"I see. Let's go in."

After showing her to her room I put the kettle on. I'd decided not to send Inma a text after all, because if the subject of my multiple conquests came up she'd surely put two and two together, as I'd told her all about my few short-lived liaisons. If I could keep Natalia occupied for an hour until she came home, she might be able to convince her not to bother the old chaps, I thought as I stirred the chamomile infusion in the pot. I heard footsteps.

"Alan, do you think there might be a homoerotic element to their cohabitation?"

I dropped the teaspoon. "No, I do not." After bending to pick it up I elected to leave my right knee in contact with the floor. "Oh, please don't bother going, Natalia! They've finally achieved a measure of harmony and I fear that your... innocuous but incisive questions might... destabilise their precarious status quo."

She sneered down at me. "Don't try to talk like an anthropologist, Alan, because you aren't one and never will be."

I leapt up, and after ruling out a deft Bogart-style blow to the chin to put her out of action until Inma came to my aid, I was foolhardy enough to challenge her credentials.

"Natalia, you're only half way through your degree, so you aren't *quite* an anthropologist yet." Her eyes flashed, but I went on. "Now, a medical student doesn't perform operations, so I want you to ask yourself if it's really ethical to enter a household in which all hell might break loose if you provoke Zefe, without meaning to, of course."

She smiled. "You may be right."

"Ah, well, let's a have a nice cup of chamomile tea and I'll tell you what we've been up to."

"But there's only one way to find out. Come on, you'll have to introduce me to them."

"Muy bien, but you'll be entirely responsible for any calamities which may occur."

"Oh, don't be so melodramatic, you silly man. I've interviewed lots of illegal immigrants in Madrid and I got on fine with them."

"Come on then."

Maybe she only loathes me, I reflected as I trudged back up to the house, because no sooner had Álvaro opened the door than she'd begun to charm the socks off him. He'd promptly led her inside without a trace of fear on his face, but I hadn't followed, oh no, preferring to close the door with me safely on the outside.

"I hope she doesn't spend the whole evening there," Inma grumbled shortly after returning home from work. I'd already told her about Wilfredo, who she assumed must be a recent acquisition, and her unbridled sex-related chatter, which didn't surprise her at all.

"She loves to tease you, Alan. You should know that by now."

"Yes, I suppose so."

She sent her daughter a text, ordering her to be back in time for supper, then we discussed our solar affairs for a while, before I showed her my new camera.

"Hmm, very nice."

I took a candid close-up from table height.

"But the flash didn't come on."

"No need, my dear, because the sensor and lens are so good that I could photograph a... a blackbird in a bin bag without a flash, I think." I switched to macro mode and snapped her left ear, her clasped hands, and her cup of microwaved chamomile.

"What on earth are you doing?"

"They're for my new project, which is still a secret."

"I see."

"Though I'll need to get a large wooden board."

"Hmm."

"About two metres by one… and a half, I think."

"Vale."

"Which I'll put on the bed in the back bedroom for now."

"OK."

"Although I should really hang it on the wall."

"As you wish."

"Aren't you dying to know what my project consists of?"

"Not if it's a secret, or it wouldn't be a secret anymore."

"That's true. It isn't that I want to keep it from you, but I'm concerned that if I try to explain it, the spontaneous nature of the undertaking may be lost."

She nodded. "Yes, I'm sure that's often the case with collages."

"Exactly… hey, how do you know it's going to be a collage?"

"You took some random shots, then mentioned a large board, so what else can it be?"

"I suppose you think it's a stupid idea."

"Not at all. In fact I believe it's ideal for a person who wishes to tap his artistic resources without quite knowing what they are."

I waited for the tinkly laugh, but it didn't come. "Seriously?"

"Yes, I think that as you proceed you'll find that ideas occur to you, so my advice is to leave the board on the bed and not to stick things to it, so you can move them around as you see fit."

"Brilliant!" I clapped. "I'm going to try out our new printer right away."

So I printed the photos I'd taken so far, cut off the boring bits, then began to arrange them on the bedspread. Inma came in to help me, and once we'd created a square foot of marvellous artwork we repaired to the dining table and began to do the jigsaw puzzle which Lars had made for me. That took about an hour, and we were half-way through Inma's puzzle when her wells of patience finally began to run dry. I suspected this was the case due to the way she slapped the pieces harshly into place, then knew for sure when she brushed the remaining bits onto the floor, thumped the table, and buried her face in her hands.

I cleared my throat in a conciliatory manner. "Er, I know it's quite difficult, dear, what with many of the pieces looking quite similar, but–"

She sat up abruptly. "It's not the puzzle, you chump, but that damned daughter of mine!" she wailed, before tears welled up in her lovely eyes and she hid them again.

"Bueno, bueno," I crooned, meaning 'there, there'. "I'm sure she'll be back soon."

Inma then wiped her eyes and made the accusatory comments you might expect, about her only child swanning off to pester two old codgers instead of catching up with her dear old mother etc. etc.

"Bueno, bueno."

"We used to be so close, then she went off to study and it's as if I've ceased to exist."

"Bueno, bueno."

"And please stop saying that. You sound like a demented owl."

"Perdona, cariño."

"Mamá! I'm back!" cried the culprit as she flung herself upon her poor old mum. "Oh, I'm sorry I'm late, but I just couldn't tear myself away."

Inma smiled at me over her clingy daughter's shoulder.

"Were they receptive then?" I said.

"Oh, they're such interesting old men, especially Zeferino." She released her mother. "I couldn't think how to start, so after telling them a little about myself I asked him about his childhood. Did you know he was brought up on a sugar plantation in Cuba?"

Inma smiled. "Er, I believe–"

"Yes, he did," I interrupted. "Though not in much detail."

"What a marvellous childhood! His parents were very rich, you see, and great friends of Batista, that nasty dictator, but Zeferino knew he was exploiting the poor, so when Fidel Castro arrived he went off to join his forces in the hills. Oh, what a time he had, freeing the peasants from that awful regime and killing as many fascist bastards as he could."

"Don't swear, dear."

"Sorry, Mamá, but his story was so exciting. Álvaro knew the whole story, of course, and was able to fill in a few bits that Zeferino had forgotten, as his memory isn't what it was. Anyway, the years he spent in the hills were nothing compared to *after* the revolution, when he became really close to Castro and Che Guevara. Just imagine, he used to beat them both at chess and they didn't mind!" She sighed. "The only trouble was that his parents had to flee to Miami. They disowned him and they'd lost most of their wealth anyway. Alan, did he tell you that he went back to their hacienda and taught the local kids how to read and write in what used to be a palatial ballroom?"

"Er, yes, I believe he did mention that."

"What a life! And you'll never guess where he went next."

I bet I can, I thought. "Er, I can't quite remember," I said.

"The Dominican Republic, where my Wilfredo's from!"

"Ah, yes, of course."

"Well, they had a nasty dictator too, called Trujillo, and after a couple of years in Havana, Fidel sent Zeferino there on a secret mission. He joined up with a group of dissidents and was driving the car when they caught that son of a bitch and shot him dead. Can you believe that?"

Inma leaned forward. "Well…"

I patted the table. "I must admit that at first I thought his stories were just a bit too incredible and I checked a few facts, but it soon became clear that he was right there in Cuba and… so on."

Natalia snorted. "That's just like you, Alan, so cynical and untrusting. Boring people always are."

I smiled this slur aside. "Remind me what he did next."

"Well, Trujillo's son soon rounded up all the conspirators and had them fed to the sharks, but Zeferino managed to swim to safety and escape." She sighed. "He had to stop speaking at that point, as he'd become ever so tired. He is ninety-three, after all, so I thought it was time to leave." She glanced at her mum. "And it was our supper time, of course."

"Hmm."

"Anyway, I gave Wilfredo a quick call to tell him the tale. He knows all about it, of course, but he's wondering what on earth Zeferino did next."

"I'm sure he'll tell you tomorrow," I said. When they've read up on it, I added to myself.

"Yes, but I can't see them until the evening. He's going to the hospital in the morning, because of the shrapnel."

"What shrap—"

I squeezed Inma's leg. "Ah, yes, the shrapnel."

Natalia grimaced and patted herself below the waist. "Right down here, so he couldn't show me the places where bits are still finding their way to the surface, poor man. That was later in Mozambique, but I can't wait for him to tell me about his time in the Dominican Republic. I may end up living there one day, after all."

Inma nodded. "So you haven't done much anthropological research, as such."

"Oh, who cares about that? I can do that boring stuff anytime. Now, tell me all about these solar panels and things."

"Let's get some supper," I said.

Later in bed I expressed approval at the way my pals were handling their visitor, but Inma was less sanguine about it. She remarked that the weekend was still young and that once Zefe's time in the Dominican Republic ended, Natalia may become bored with his stories, or begin to disbelieve them.

"Then, if she feels she's been misled, she might turn on them and upset their harmonious cohabitation, as you call it, or simply hurry back and spend the rest of her time here sulking. Either way, I doubt it'll be the pleasant visit I'd hoped for. You must call Álvaro in the morning."

"Why?"

"Oh, to see how they mean to proceed. She's staying till Tuesday and if she spends the whole time with them I won't be happy."

"Hmm, I shall sleep on it and see if I dream up one of my bright ideas."

"You do that."

11

The next morning while Natalia was telling her mother all about Wilfredo, I slipped out and scampered down to Álvaro's house. I found Zefe reading aloud from a history book while his friend made notes. The problem with the post-Trujillo Dominican Republic, Álvaro told me, was that it was ever so complicated, their being several changes of leadership, a civil war, and an American occupation, followed by a boring decade of stability.

"It's interesting in itself, but makes far less appealing story material than Cuba, with its famous figures who even semi-educated youngsters have heard of."

Zefe slapped shut the book. "Bah, and it's too easy. She laps it up and never asks any challenging questions, as you used to do. It's nice to have a pretty girl hanging on my every word, but I can't keep it up for much longer." He patted his lower torso. "That's why I'm having my shrapnel attended to today, to give us a break."

I smiled. "Good thinking. She believed that too."

After debating the issue for a while we agreed that fatigue would overtake Zefe once he'd covered the sixties, and that any further meetings would be relatively short ones, so that Inma would also see something of her daughter. Out on the street Álvaro asked me why I feared that the charming girl might upset their precious status quo, or entente cordiale, as he liked to call it.

"Oh, I don't know. I'm beginning to think it's only me she likes to rile." When he laughed I spotted a gold filling. "Er, has he mentioned the Sierra Pelada recently?"

"Not much. Since I threatened him with banishment to his flat he's behaved in an exemplary manner, most of the time." He took my arm and led me away from the flaky door. "But the little he's said has made me believe that there may be some truth in it after all, especially after his startling declaration once Natalia had left last night."

"What was that?"

"Well, first he said that my car was a lamentable heap of junk and an embarrassment for him to be driven around in."

"Hmm, and I can't lend you the Clio much now."

"Then he told me he's going to buy me a new one."

"Really?"

"Yes. I thanked him quietly, fearing it to be one of his little jokes, but he declared that on Monday morning we are to drive to Elda, leave my loathsome little Peugeot at the dealership, and drive home in a brand new Citroen Berlingo."

I gasped. "Wow! Brand new, but why a Berlingo?"

He smiled. "Because they can easily be adapted to admit wheelchairs, so if his legs cease to function I'll still be able to take him out and about. That's the principal condition of his gift, you see, that we begin to take more trips, to the seaside and suchlike. As you can imagine, I gladly agreed to this, and now my only concern is that he may change his mind before then. So far Natalia has improved his mood, but I need to maintain his high spirits during the whole weekend." He sighed. "And I fear that more storytelling may not be enough."

Even since he'd mentioned the new car my mind had been working like the blazes, as I too feared a change of heart, but the idea I came up with surpassed even my habitual brilliance. On hearing it he clasped his hands and hopped from foot to foot.

"Oh, yes, yes, yes! That would be perfect. It'll show him what we're missing and on Monday the Berlingo will undoubtedly be mine. Just imagine, a brand new car. I've never had one before. You're a genius, Alan!"

I shrugged with my habitual modesty, before going home to tell Inma about my selfless brainwave. Luckily her daughter was in the shower.

"Oh, no, no, no!" my wife wailed.

"But it's something we've promised ourselves to do more often, love."

"Yes, but not with that tiresome old man."

By the time Natalia emerged I'd persuaded her that going to the seaside with Zefe was better than not going at all, and would ensure a whole day with her daughter, who might otherwise ensconce herself with the oldies for hours on end.

"Oh, all right."

"What's that, Mamá?"

She told her.

"Oh, that's great! I can't wait."

"But now I must go to the bar for a few hours, as both Alicia and Randi are off and they won't manage without me."

I clucked a few times. "I won't hear of it. I'll go instead."

"Alan now works there occasionally, you see," Inma explained.

Natalia eyed me scornfully. "Him?"

"Yes, me. I'm a fast-improving apprentice waiter, I'll have you know."

"Then I'm going too. Whatever he can do, I can do *far* better."

Inma smiled. "You two go along while I paint for a while. I'll be there for lunch."

"Served by your loving husband."

"No, served by your loving daughter. Stop dithering, Alan. We've got work to do."

The great thing about Natalia's single-mindedness – bordering on tunnel vision – is that her current enthusiasm expels all other thoughts from her mind, so during the short drive I suffered no sex talk or any other form of teasing, just a fervent desire for me to bring her up to speed before she walked through the door. On doing so she made straight for a recently vacated table and began to clear up, I observed from the other side of the bead curtain.

"Hey, who are you?" Jorge wailed from behind the bar.

"Natalia," she snapped. "Give me a damp cloth."

On hearing Rosa's explanatory tones I found myself shuffling away, feeling that the bar wasn't quite big enough for the both of us. As it was sunny I decided to walk over to my sister's, but only made it as far as Bernie's field, where he proudly showed me the slightly larger olive trees on his still weedless field. After he'd lamented the lack of real rain during the past month, I attempted to recruit him for our imminent expedition.

"Sorry, Alan, but Cathy can't stand that foul-mouthed old fart."

"Then appeal to her charitable side. Álvaro's new car may depend on a successful outing, and the five of us riding coastwards in Inma's Ibiza is far from ideal. If you two come we'll be able to share the burden and ensure a splendid time is had by one and all."

"She won't buy it, mate."

"And I'll tell you something else. Álvaro reckons that the Brazil business might be true, not least because Zefe intends to pay for the car with his new bank card."

Bernie pushed back his straw hat. "At least twenty grand in his current account, eh?"

"Exactly. So just imagine how much he might have stashed away elsewhere."

"You're on. If Cathy can't face him, she can stay here." He grabbed my arm. "And when you inherit we'll remind her of her lack of solidarity, eh?"

"Yes, Bernie. We'll be at yours before ten. Oh, Natalia's at the bar, by the way."

"Then let's go and see the little darling."

"Not yet. We'll all go for lunch, on me."

Seeing Natalia bustling around the bar wearing a pretty apron over her sweater and jeans reminded me of our first ever meeting, when she'd subjected me to a lengthy and critical interrogation regarding my suitability as her mother's partner. On that occasion she'd worked enthusiastically too, but today it was a joy to watch her barking orders at the hapless Jorge as she buzzed from table to table with pad in hand and a smile from ear to ear.

"Maybe she's discovering her untapped servility as I did," I said in English as we tucked into Rosa's delicious Fideuà, a paella-type dish made with pasta instead of rice.

"She's a bit bossy," Bernie said. "I wouldn't like to be in the bloke's shoes who ends up with her." He looked her up and down. "Although guess I'd be able to hack it for a while."

Cathy growled, Inma laughed, and I set about giving my sister a pep talk regarding the seaside jaunt she wasn't looking forward to one bit. I promised that she wouldn't have to ride with the obnoxious old ogre – her words – and that we ought to take the opportunity, as a family unit, to check out at least one place where Inma and I might end up donning our straw hats and settling down to enjoy our autumn years. Inma had suggested a few places which might or might not appeal to us, as with the exception of Águilas and Alicante she hadn't knocked about on the coast for many a year, so I intended to employ my analytical skills to hone in on the ideal spot for our future home, five to ten years hence.

"It'll be like a foreign country to me," said Bernie, flexing his toil-hardened hands.

"It is a foreign country," said Cathy.

"To you, maybe, but when you've laboured on the land for long enough you begin to feel at one with it."

I chuckled. "You'll soon become a tree-hugger, Bern."

"Ah, I hope I live long enough to embrace my olive trees like I embrace Cathy here, but I believe they take up to a hundred years to reach their maximum girth." Cathy frowned. "No joke intended, love. Yes, and they usually live for about five hundred years, although they reckon some have been around for well over a thousand. Ah, it makes you realise how insignificant us humans are, just passing through, and buggering things up more and more as we go."

Cathy yawned.

"Which subtly brings me onto the subject of solar power and whatnot."

I pricked up my recently unresponsive ears, as I'd heard all Bernie's whimsical nature talk before.

He knocked back half a glass of white wine. "I really thought that my salesman days were behind me, as I made my pile flogging motors and felt no desire to amass more wealth."

"Er, I worked for thirty-odd years too," said Cathy.

"So you did, love, and in an honourable profession, tending to the sick while I just helped to fill the air with more carbon-bloody-monoxide, and now you visit your oldies, making their waning years more… more… less crap. Yes, your life has been and still is one of solidarity with your fellow man, but what have I done?"

"Get to the point, Bern."

"I'd like to have a go at selling solar stuff too."

I scratched my chin. "Oh..."

"That's brilliant, Bernie," said Inma.

I raised a finger. "Er..."

Inma grasped his hand. "Welcome to the team. When can you start?"

"Well, whenever my labours permit it, which is most of the time right now." He looked at me. "But I only want to do a bit. You know, maybe visiting the Brit punters who you think might be tough nuts to crack."

"Alan's strength is driving around and leaving the leaflets," said Inma. "He's very good at that and he enjoys it, don't you, Alan?"

I shrugged. "Yes, but–"

"He is also a great salesman."

"Is he?" said Bernie.

"Am I?" said I.

"Yes, but selling coins on the computer is your main strength. Selling to... physical people is Bernie's strength." She squeezed his hand. "Ah, now with you I feel that our team is complete. Three people who know exactly what they have to do."

I sniffed haughtily. "Yes, but remember, dear, that the more people who are involved, the less for each of us. It's elementary arithmetic."

They all had a good laugh about this, including the hovering Natalia, so I joined in, fearing a wounding barb from the feisty waitress. Having Bernie to tackle the British customers was a great boost, of course, although Inma's instant ebullience had dented my self-esteem, but not for long, because after lunch I was soon on the phone to Fran, informing him of the new addition to our solar squad.

"Sí, sí, that's a marvellous idea, Alan!"

I held the phone away and stuck out my tongue. "But you only met Bernie briefly, Fran."

"I know, but I can spot a true salesman from a kilometre away."

"I see."

Pregnant pause.

"Yes, and I can also spot a great organiser, Alan, which is what you are."

"Am I?"

"Of course. Don't you see? Yes, in no time at all you've recruited two ideal people to strengthen your team. What vision! I wish I had that ability but, alas, for the moment I have to soldier on alone."

"How many sales have you made so far?"

"Six, but nearer the coast I think it's easier than up there. There's more money, more foreigners and even more sunlight, but I'm sure with your recent recruits you'll soon surpass me."

"What did you use to do before, Fran?"

"Me? Oh, I was in the army, then I worked in an office, then I began to sell. So, good luck and let me know if they install your friend's panels on Monday. I believe they will."

"Yes. What did you sell?"

"Oh, crema para he...r...des," he mumbled.

"Crema para qué?"

He cleared his throat. "Haemorrhoid cream."

"Ah, right."

He sighed. "Yes, a friend persuaded me to try my hand at selling an exclusive product from Switzerland, now discontinued in Spain, but not due to my incompetence. It proved to be a very difficult and somewhat embarrassing product to sell, but I learnt a lot, chiefly about human nature, and it whetted my appetite for sales, so I then chose a more sensible field in which to work."

"A tough apprenticeship."

"Exactly, but now we're all going to make lots of money, so they can stick their haemorrhoid cream up their arse, ha ha. Keep in touch, Alan, and good luck."

"You too, Fran."

That evening Natalia returned from Álvaro's house in a far more subdued state than the previous day. It turned out that Zefe, having wished to keep a low profile after playing his part in murdering the Dominican dictator, had grown a beard and spent a few years fishing in a tiny village on the northern coast, before flying back to Europe and thence to Mozambique, where he worked as an overseer at a small copper mine.

"So his shrapnel wasn't from a war, but from a blast that went wrong. He came home to recover, then worked at a marble quarry until he retired, so Cuba and the assassination were the high points in an otherwise uneventful life."

Nicely done, I thought.

She sighed. "Then Álvaro began to tell me about his school-teaching days and I couldn't stop yawning." She looked at me. "Still, at least Zeferino did something exciting in his life, unlike some people."

"I formed part of an undercover team in the Falklands conflict and was among the first to enter Port Stanley, but even now I'm not allowed to talk about it."

She tutted contemptuously. "I wasn't born yesterday, Alan."

I smiled. "Of course you weren't, dear."

"I'm not your dear."

"No, Natalia."

About an hour after departing from Cathy and Bernie's house, Zefe began to complain of claustrophobia, despite sitting beside me in the Ibiza with the seat pushed back, as only Inma sat in the rear, with her earphones inserted ever since we'd set off.

"The Berlingo will be far more spacious," I said.

"I bloody hope so. What are we doing on the motorway anyway?"

I explained that rather than visiting the boring old Alicante coast, we were going to check out a small town where Inma and I might choose to live one day. I told him that after a painstaking process of elimination I'd concluded that all nearby places were too infested by foreigners and/or lacked interesting landscape for Inma to paint.

"So we're nipping down here. Ah, what a lovely day! Look, seventeen degrees and we're still heading south. Ooh, look at the mountains up ahead."

"It's getting drier all the time."

"Hmm, yes, I've noticed that. Still, by the seaside one looks out to sea, from the marvellous cliffs I've seen on the computer. Yes, I'm still confident that San Juan de los Terrenos will be ideal for us, as I didn't burn the midnight oil for nothing."

He grunted. "Is it far?"

"No, not so far now."

"A hundred and seventy kilometres and we end up in this shithole," Bernie declared on our arrival at about noon.

"It's not so bad. Look at the palm trees, and we've passed some pretty houses."

"And some horrible ones, half of them for sale," said Cathy. "And it's practically a desert around here."

"It's the easternmost town in Andalucia," I said with all eyes upon me. "With craggy cliffs to paint," I added weakly.

Imna squeezed my hand. "It isn't so bad, compared to some other places on this coast."

Bernie snorted. "Er, Inma, aren't you forgetting Javea, Denia, Altea and places like that? I've seen lovely houses in proper woodland near Javea."

"They cost a fortune, Bern. I've checked."

He grinned. "Don't forget that I've joined the team now, mate. We'll soon be making money hand over fist."

"We're talking hundreds of thousands in Javea."

"You've got five or ten years to make them. Where there's a will there's a way."

For some reason I pictured Malcolm, who I hadn't heard from for a while.

"Our aspirations are more modest, Bernie," said Inma.

He looked up and down the wide, dusty avenue where not a little litter was blowing around in the breeze. "Yeah, but there's a limit."

"Speak Spanish!" Zefe cried, raising his right-hand stick.

I thin… thought you lived in Detroit one time," Bernie said in that language.

"I've forgotten my English." He jabbed his stick in a seaward direction. "To the beach!"

As we all understood that our principle mission was to maintain Zefe's high spirits, his wish was our command, so on the longish beach Bernie and I soon lowered him onto a small folding chair and levered off his shoes, while Inma fetched him a glass of wine and a bottle of water from a nearby bar. Álvaro and Natalia remained close by to cater to any further whims, while Cathy and Bernie went for a walk along the shoreline, so Inma and I wandered off to tour the higgledy-piggledy town, if only to see how we'd feel about living in such a place, she said. After visiting the lacklustre Sunday market, where Spaniards just about outnumbered foreigners, we jumped in the car and soon felt deflated by the residential architecture – mostly low-rise apartments and terraces of strikingly ugly holiday homes – so we headed up to the small and thoroughly restored castle from where Inma summed up the area's artistic potential.

"I guess I'd paint that little island, the headlands and those cliffs, but it's all so dry that I'd soon get bored of it."

I nodded glumly. "I suppose I chose a pretty poor place to visit really. It sounded better on paper, and looked more picturesque in the photos."

"Oh, it's no worse than most other seaside towns in the south. Ah, do you remember Lastres?"

"How could I forget it? It's another world."

"We must frame the painting that Juanje sent us."

"Yes, and visit him in the spring, because I doubt he'll come to ours, now that he's busy seeing his sons again."

She chuckled. "Asturias has corrupted us. Look along the coast, and inland at the mountains, and imagine it all covered in trees."

"Yes, and the red-roofed villages only tainted by tourism in summer, and few foreigners even then. Are you thinking what I'm thinking, cariño?"

"I think so, but with my parents in Murcia... well, we'll see how things go. One oughtn't to live for the future, after all."

"No. I must write to Juanje soon though, lest he forget us."

"He won't."

I'd like to report the odd episode of Zefe or Natalia-related high jinks, but I can't because they behaved themselves and a pleasant time was had by all. After a passable seafood paella we returned to the beach to soak up the remaining rays until the temperature plummeted and we made for the cars. Álvaro joined

Zefe and me for the return trip and while the old man snoozed we assessed the state of play regarding the Berlingo which my neighbour had now set his heart on.

"I think we'll find out when he wakes up," he said from the back. "He never ceases to cogitate during his slumbers and I hope that his pleasant time in the sun will outweigh the tiresome hours in the car."

Fortunately we were almost home when he began to mumble and drool.

"Not far now, Zefe," I murmured.

He slowly opened his eyes. "I'm dry."

Álvaro handed him a small bottle.

He sipped and smacked his lips. "Mm, what's this?"

"Half water, half wine."

He took a long swig. "Ah, very refreshing."

"Have you enjoyed the outing?" I asked him.

"Hmm, mostly."

"It's good to get out and about, isn't it?"

"Sí." He tapped the roof. "But not in this sardine can."

"It is quite a small car, I suppose."

"Tiny." He gazed out of the window for a while. "Our Berlingo will be much better."

"Of course it will." I glanced in the mirror and saw Álvaro's clenched fists on either side of his beaming face.

12

Then I became ever so busy. The following day I worked fairly harmoniously in the bar with Natalia while Inma went off to follow a couple of solar leads, and after her daughter's departure on Tuesday I resumed my leafleting campaign, secured a sale to the Chippenham couple after they'd seen Jesús's nifty installation, bought a George I shilling for a song, took a few photos for my collage, and went for a quick spin in Álvaro's shiny blue Berlingo. Meanwhile Inma's lawyer proceeded with the house sale, so we had to start looking for a rental property right away.

"Unless we finally decide to buy," she said on Friday evening, as pleased as punch after making her first sale. Bernie already had one in the pipeline too, so we felt confident and content as we sat sipping a nice Rueda white wine and nibbling cheese and crackers.

"Er, might we decide to buy then?"

She shrugged. "Let's not rule it out just yet. If we hear about a place that suits us, we ought to consider it."

"Are you, er… plotting something, dear?"

"Me? Of course not. Luckily Liz and Rob are quite flexible about their moving date, but we wouldn't want to hold them back for more than a fortnight."

"No." I observed her obliquely, my left eye shaded by a cracker.

"And we can always stay at Cathy and Bernie's for a while if we have too."

"Ah."

"And store our things in a big garage that Rosa's uncle doesn't use."

Sure that she had something up her sleeve, I decided to employ all my cunning in order to elicit a clue or two. "That would be a lot of hassle though. No, I shall visit the agencies next week and see what they've got to rent."

"By all means make enquiries."

"I will, and I'll see if they've got anything new for sale too."

"You do that, if you can spare the time. I know I can't."

Still clueless, I tried another tactic, heralded by a bout of yawning. "Ah, I can't either really, what with loads of leafleting still to do to lay the groundwork for you two hotshots, and coins to buy and... things. Maybe we should just wait and see if anyone knocks on the door, offering us a house."

She performed a genuine yawn, I think. "Whatever. Look, let's not do anything for a fortnight, then we'll just go out and find somewhere."

Given the uncharacteristic laxity of her approach to such a pressing matter, I was now convinced that her sleeve was positively bulging with a strong candidate for our next abode, but as I like a mystery as much as the next man, if not more, I decided to postpone all house-hunting until she lost her nerve and spilled the beans. Besides, there were worse fates than ending up at my sister's for a while, as then I'd have two great cooks in residence, plus an even better one just a few minutes' walk away.

"Is Randi settling in all right?" I asked.

Inma coughed. "Excuse me. At home or at the bar?"

"Both."

"She's always enjoyed working at the bar, and I believe she and Arvid are getting along fairly well." She smiled. "Did you take any more photos today?"

Suddenly remembering my artistic aspirations, I scurried off to get my camera.

The next fortnight passed by in a blur of unprecedented activity for me. No sooner did I finish a strenuous leafleting tour than Inma would summon me to the bar while she hurtled off to beguile a potential punter. This happened almost every day, and as Bernie was busy too I had no end of paperwork to complete of an evening, so my coin-dealing was put on hold once again. Despite Inma's fears, or hopes, I suffered no upsets during my waitering hours and any slight rudeness I encountered was brushed off like an insignificant bit of dandruff, because we were beginning to make so much money with the panels – but not turbines, alas – that I simply felt sorry for the odd irate workman and trotted off to change his cold coffee or flat beer.

When I began to dream of marbled halls, enormous windows and infinity pools – a new aspiration – Inma pointed out that the initial rush of orders was unlikely to last, so I oughtn't to imagine that we could afford to spend more than €180,000 on a house, at the most.

"Ha!" I cried. "I've got you now!"

She rubbed her ears then sipped her tea. "What have I done?"

"You've given yourself away, that's what you've done. These last two weeks I've been waiting for you to crack, and now you have, a bit."

"I don't understand."

"Look, you know as well as I do that we should be desperately seeking a house by now, as in less than a month Liz and Rob will want to move in, but you've calmly gone about your business as if there were all the time in the world."

She sighed. "But we'll be able to stay at Cathy and Bernie's if we have to."

"No, no, no. I mean, yes, of course we can, but that price you just mentioned suggests that you've got your eye on something specific. Now all I have to do is find out what it is."

Another sigh. "It isn't so simple, Alan. Look, I'll try to explain things without saying too much, because your ignorance of proceedings is essential for my plan to succeed."

"Eh? Why?"

"It just is. It's true that I have my eye on a certain property… but no, it's no good, I can't give you any clues at all. I can only say that it's a sensitive situation in which more than one person's wellbeing has to be considered. Right now negotiations are afoot which don't involve me much, but if anyone were to interfere, the whole thing could be cancelled, such is the nature of a certain… element. Is that clear?"

"Yes, as clear as Jorge's dishwater."

"Hmm, we must tell him to empty the sink more often."

"Don't try to change the subject."

She took my hand. "Just give me another week, Alan. If nothing has come of it by then I'll tell you all about it. I think you'll then understand why I've had to keep you out of it."

"Is it because you don't think I can keep a secret?"

"Yes. I mean, you might manage to keep it, but it'll be bursting to get out, which may become evident, and you might be tempted to snoop, which could spoil the whole thing or put the house beyond our reach."

I grasped my head and moaned. "Oh, on top of everything I have to think about, now you torment me with this awful riddle!"

"Bueno, bueno, try to put it out of your mind for just a few days."

"All right, I'll try. Hey, and what if I don't like this mystery house?"

She smiled. "I'm almost sure you will. It has… certain characteristics which will please us."

I feigned another yawn. "Hmm, whereabouts is it?"

"In Spain. Now have another glass of wine and try to relax."

"Fat chance," I said in English.

The worst thing that could have happened just then would have been to receive a call from Malcolm telling me that Operation Hotel Sale had to be put into action right away. Luckily fate seldom deals such cruel blows, so when bedtime arrived I'd calmed down and become resigned to biding my time until Inma chose to enlighten me.

My mobile rang at eight the next morning, so I jumped out of bed and hurried into the living room, thinking it might be an especially eager customer.

"Hello, Alan Laycock speaking," I said as cheerily as a man who'd been up and about for hours.

"Hello, Alan Laycock," said Malcolm. "Operation Hotel Sale has to be put into action right away, so get your arse over here double quick."

"But... but I've got work to do."

"Too right. Be here by nine, and bring Inma if she can make it." He hung up and I went wailing back to the bedroom to tell her the awful news.

Rather than fobbing me off, she sat up straight away. "Come on, you big baby, opportunity is knocking on the door."

"I'm not his damned servant, to be summoned at the drop of a... a telephone call." Inma got up and walked briskly to the bathroom. "And neither are you," I said, hot on her heels.

"I know I'm not. I'm coming because I wish to ensure that you're rewarded for this job of work, as promised. Twenty to thirty thousand was the figure he mentioned, I believe."

"Yes, well, he was in a good mood at the time."

"I mean to hold him to his word. That money might be crucial if that house proves..." She groaned.

"Go on, go on!"

She slid her hand across my forehead. "Please wipe that lapsus linguae from your mind."

"That what? Oh, slip of the tongue, right."

"And close the door behind you."

So it was that at 8.59am we parked up outside the hotel, near the Land Cruiser, the Hymer, Arturo's rusty old van and a dusty Dacia Duster.

"No guests, by the look of it," I said.

"Al-an! In-ma!" Arturo cried from the doorway, before swaggering over. While he was kissing Inma I positioned my forearm in an upright position, but he held his straight out. We shook.

"I'm using the payo (non-gypsy) handshake now, Alan, and look." He held up both hands.

"Oh, no rings."

"No. I fear I'll soon be returning to the markets, but this Dutch guy who might buy the hotel seems to like me, so I'm hoping he'll give me a job. He isn't a cool dude like you though, so I'm getting used to behaving like a full-on payo."

I smiled. "You could cut your hair."

He grasped his ponytail. "Oh, no, not that."

He led us into the lounge and I asked him if the prospective buyer had already arrived.

"Not here. He flew into Alicante yesterday, so Malc and me raced down to the airport in the Cruiser."

I pulled my right earlobe. "Did you say Malc?"

"Sí."

"Does he let you call him that?" I said, as even I used the diminutive sparingly, if at all.

"Course he does. He calls me Art, so I call him Malc."

"And Angela?"

"Angela," he said with the soft Spanish G. "She's in England now, looking for a new place to spend their money on."

Angela's absence didn't sadden me too much, because I still felt guilty about having bailed out of the hotel so soon after it had opened.

"This is ever so interesting," said Inma. "But shouldn't we find Malcolm and get down to business?"

"I think he's having a bath."

I snorted indignantly, having bolted my breakfast in order to arrive on time.

"But I'm to fill you in. This Dutch guy was going to hire a car and come straight here, but Malc didn't want that, of course, as there are no guests, so even though the guy says he wants to make the place into some sort of sanatorium, it'd still look bad if it was empty. So, we picked him up and Malc started telling him how great the place is and before the guy knew it we'd arrived at the best hotel in Elda and I was carrying his bags inside. He was a bit confused, but you know how Malc is. When he talks, you just listen, and he then tells the guy that his hotel is full up and he wouldn't dream of taking him there without being able to show him every single room. Luckily, he tells him, it's a huge party of ornithologists who're having a conference and they're all leaving today, so he's going to shift the new guests to another hotel he's got near Jumilla. That way the guy can have the place to himself, you see."

"And did the guy (tío, as in uncle) believe that incredible story?" Inma asked him.

"I think so. Malc's very convincing."

"That's true," I said. "So when is he coming?"

"I'm to pick him up at six. Malc told him he couldn't possibly come till the whole place had been cleaned."

"Right, so what am I... are we supposed to do?"

He grinned. "Malc's gonna tell you that."

The big man soon appeared, looking relatively trim in a shiny blue tracksuit and white trainers.

I shaded my eyes. "Morning, Malc...olm. You're looking sporty."

"Yes." He nodded at Inma. "Hello, love. Yes, I think better in this gear, and we've got some serious thinking to do. Art, get Celia to make us some coffee."

"OK, Malc." He left.

"He's a good lad that one. I'll miss him." He sat down. "Right, so this Dutch fella reckons he wants to set up some poncy sanatorium and it sounds like he's got plenty of money behind him, but he's not happy about the price. I'm asking eight-hundred grand, but he's saying he'll pay seven-thirty tops, and that's no good to us, is it?"

"No, Malcolm. You said you wanted seven-fifty."

"Yep, but I guess I can sort the agency's commission out of that, and as you two are going to help me pull this off, any extra will be for you."

I scratched my head. "Er..."

"What do you have in mind, Malcolm?" Inma said serenely.

"Right, well, as I've spun him that yarn about shifting my new guests, we just need to have plenty of staff buzzing around. I'll need a top-notch chef too, as Celia's not even a proper cook. So, we show him around the impeccable rooms, then give him a first class dinner and plenty of wine." He tapped his right temple. "But something in here tells me that won't be enough, so I need ideas and I need them quick."

Arturo returned with the coffee tray. "I say to Malc I can get a flamenco group, but he think that no good for this man."

Malcolm shook his head. "No, he's a real po-faced bugger. Came dressed in a suit too, the pillock. I suspect he's representing some big-shot and I reckon this sanatorium business might be a lot of baloney, but that's neither here nor there. We need some sort of... stimulus to make him up his offer. So, folks, what's it to be?"

Have you ever had a bright idea that becomes obsolete as the conversation moves on but which you can't resist airing anyway? I bet you can't beat this one.

"I think we should leave some ornithology magazines lying around," I said, causing six eyes to stare at me. "It adds verisimilitude to the story about the departed guests, you see." Silence. "Little details like that can make all the difference." Sighs. "Sometimes."

Malcolm appeared to shake a touch of fuzziness from his head, then clapped. "Inma, it looks like I'm going to have to depend on you."

"Right, we can close the bar this afternoon and all come here. Randi is a great cook and Jorge can help her. Rosa and I can look busy and later serve the meal. Alan can sit very quietly in reception. More staff would look strange, as you would naturally give most of them a free day after such a busy week."

"That's true. Yes, thanks, so that's all the basic stuff covered."

She smiled. "Then we need another guest, or guests."

"Uh-huh."

"Someone else who is interested to buy the hotel."

"In buying the hotel," I murmured.

"Shut up, birdbrain," said Malcolm without deigning to look at me. "That idea's crossed my mind too. I'd even thought of roping in Wanker to do the job, but the slimy git would want a slice of the pie and I'm not having that." He beamed at Inma. "I'm fairly sure I can get seven-fifty out of the Dutchman, but I did promise that husband of yours an opportunity to make a bit of cash, so here we are."

She smiled sweetly. "We're grateful for that, Malcolm. Now, let me think. Who can we get so quickly? Certain local people occur to me, but I think another foreigner might be more convincing. Alan's brother-in-law is an astute man and Cathy could accompany him, but I don't think they're quite right for this job. Hmm, then there's the couple who are going to buy our house, but no, they are modest, middle-class people and I think we need someone more... who will have more impact."

"I can bring a big old gypsy man who wear lots of gold," said Arturo.

"Thanks, but no thanks, Art."

"Álvaro?" I ventured timidly.

"He looks too poor, even with his new car," said Inma.

"Oh, there's got to be someone," Malcolm muttered.

I uttered a strangled cry, before finding my voice. "The Belgians! Yes, yes, Lars and Nina, especially Lars!" I stared ecstatically at Malcolm. "He's a very striking man, very cultured, and a great linguist, as is Nina, and above all they're Belgians. The Belgians and the Dutch are bound to be great rivals, them being neighbours, so that could provide just the stimulus we need."

"Might they do, Inma?" Malcolm asked.

"Hmm, I think so, but I'm not sure they'll have suitable clothes. They now reject their old lives, you see, although they are clearly very cosmopolitan."

He glanced at his gold wristwatch. "Clothes can be bought in a jiffy, but I'll need to see these people."

"They live about half an hour from here," I said.

He stood up. "Come on then. The Hymer needs a run anyway."

My brilliant wife then suggested we also take her Ibiza. "Their jeep is very old and won't create the right impression. If you think they're good for the job, they could drive here in the Hymer, so it seems they are touring around, looking for the right place to buy."

"Great idea. Art, you'll follow us in Inma's car."

"OK, Malc."

Once Malcolm had powered away along the drive I took out my phone, intending to warn Lars about the shock they were about to receive, but Inma told me not to.

"I think it'll be best, love." I tapped my gnashers to indicate the gap in Lars' teeth.

"No, I think they will like a surprise and a challenge."

"I only hope our friend here isn't too surprised," I murmured in Spanish.

A while later I told Malcolm to pull up in front of the gate.

"Looks like a decent place. Oh, what the fu... hell is all that stuff?"

"They're artists," I said, sure that Inma had been wrong about not allowing me to warn them. "Lars! Nina!" I hollered through the gate.

"Hola, Alan! Just push it open," he hollered back.

Buck, the foxy Alsatian, came to greet us politely and led the way around the house, where we found Lars wielding a blowtorch. Nina was holding a pair of bicycle forks above a structure consisting of a great jumble of things, including a small metal sink, part of a lawnmower, sundry coat hangers, more bike parts, a rusty barbecue, a pitchfork and, more or less in the centre of all this, a large revolving globe.

"Just a moment, amigos," said Lars, before roughly welding the forks to two pitchfork prongs. "There, that's it."

"Hey, you crazy guy!" said Arturo, never a stickler for etiquette. "Where are your gloves and goggles?"

"Oh, it was just a quick weld." He surveyed us for the first time. "Introduce us, Alan."

"This is Arturo," I said in English. "And this is Malcolm, who has an interesting proposition for you."

Lars gave him a gap-toothed grin. "You look like a sporty old fellow. Do you want to take a swim?" he said in an English accent every bit as good as mine.

I expected a ghastly glower and terse orders to beat a retreat from this den of weirdos, but he bestowed a charming smile upon the scruffy couple. "Another time, perhaps. Alan thinks you may be able to help us with a very tricky matter, and for some reason I'm beginning to believe it."

"I dunno, Malc," said the still perturbed Arturo. "Maybe that Juanca is better after all."

"No wankers!"

Nina laughed.

"But what's this?" I said, distracted from our task by the hideous structure.

"Oh, it's our first attempt at a sculpture. As you can probably guess, it represents the state of the world due to man's presence upon it," she said in English. "It's pretty awful, but one has to start somewhere."

I looked at Malcolm. "They take abstract photos too."

"But there's no time to talk about that now," said Inma.

Lars pointed up the slope. "When are we getting our turbines, Alan?"

"Next week."

"Come inside and I'll make some tea," said Nina.

We were soon seated in the cluttered lounge, listening to Malcolm's explanation of the situation, followed by a scathing description of the strait-laced Dutchman.

"The tedious twerp has no idea that other possible buyers are coming, so it'll come as a shock. The question is, what kind of a shock are we going to give him?" A mighty index finger shot towards me. "Alan, your ideas first."

"Er, well, if Lars has a shave and puts in his denture and maybe brushes his hair down and wears nice clothes, and if Nina wears a modest but stylish dress, I think they might look like well-off folk arriving in their posh motorhome, so then it's just a question of how to convince the Dutchman that they really have the will and the... wherewithal to buy the place."

"A sound idea, Alan."

I shrugged. "Thanks."

"But it won't do. It's far too obvious, and not much fun. Any ideas, Art?"

He shook his head. "Don't ask me, Malc. Nothing of this make no sense to me."

"Inma?"

Her eyes alighted on Lars' mop of frizzy hair. "Hmm, if we wanted a conventional approach, I don't think we would choose Lars and Nina. I think we must use their unusuality..."

"Unusualness," I couldn't help but murmur.

"Shush, you," said M.

"...use their unusualness to our advantage. So, we have two Belgian eccentrics who arrive at the hotel in an expensive vehicle. So far so good, but how can they really convince the Dutchman that they are able to buy such a big place?"

Nina stood up. "Excuse me a moment. I'm going to change into something I could wear later." Giggling softly, she toddled off.

"Will you be able to wind up the Dutchman, Lars?" I said. "Do you have jokes about each other?"

"Well, the Dutch pretend to think that we Belgians are stupid, while we consider them tight-fisted." He shrugged. "I could tell a few Dutchman jokes, but I'm not sure they'd help."

"Tell us a good 'un while we're waiting," said Malcolm.

He smiled. "OK, here's a Dutch newspaper story. Collision between two taxis – twenty-three people hurt."

We chuckled, before explaining it to Arturo.

"And something else about the Dutch. Why do Belgians book island holidays? So they won't see Dutch motorhomes. Ha, the Dutchman who's coming might even have his own Hymer. They fill them to the roof with food, you see, then tour Europe for a month and spend about ten euros. Hey, maybe we'll buy the hotel just to spite the waardeloze nederlander."

"The what?" I asked.

"The lousy Dutchman."

"It's a bit expensive, Lars. Over €750,000, we hope."

His smile suggested they might manage that at a pinch, then Nina waltzed in wearing a hippyish dress of various pastel shades, a pair of stout boots, and lots of artificial jewellery, including an absurd tiara perched atop her mussed up hair. She paraded around the room, swishing her dress from side to side, before halting before the fireplace.

"So what do you think of me? Be honest now."

Arturo covered his eyes and shook his head.

"It may be a bit over the top," I said. "Don't you think so, Inma?"

"I… I don't know. There's something about–"

The sofa screeched as Malcolm pushed himself up, before striding robotically towards Nina. He stopped and folded his arms.

"Is it real, love?"

"Yes."

"That's brilliant!" He turned to face us, shaking his great fists with glee. "Bloody brilliant!"

"Is what real?" I said.

"Think, you chump."

"I know," said Inma.

"Real Doctor Martens boots?" said Arturo.

Lars grinned. "And remember, he's a Dutchman. They know about these things. Well done, Nina."

She bowed low, before removing the tiara with a flourish.

"I've got it!" I cried.

"Well done, Einstein," said Malcolm. "Let's have a look, love." She handed him the tiara. "Hmm, these are old-cut and this row's rose-cut. Angela knows more about diamonds than me, but even I can tell it's worth a bloody fortune. Is it an heirloom?"

"Yes, on my mother's side. We keep it in the safe, but it'll be lovely to wear it just this once."

He cackled. "And the great things is, with all that other crap you're wearing, it might take the Dutchy a while to twig, but when he does, oh boy, is he going to crap his pants, assuming he's representing someone else, and if he isn't he'll know that he's up against some serious competitors."

"Er, would it be too crass to ask how much it's worth?" I asked.

"Yes," said Inma.

Nina shrugged. "I'm not sure, but at least fifty thousand, I think."

"More than that," said Lars. "Hmm, now, what shall I wear?"

"The scruffier the better, mate," said Malcolm. "It's all about impact, you see. Throwing him off his guard, shaking him up. Hmm, it might be best if you meet him without the tiara, love, then pop it on before dinner." He sipped his tea. "Those sparkling stones alone won't do it though. We need a plan of action."

So we settled down to create one.

13

When Arturo arrived with the disgruntled Dutchman shortly after seven, the Hymer was sitting squarely in front of the main entrance, while several modest cars were parked in the shadows. As the newcomer sat in the Land Cruiser, poking his phone, Arturo rushed over to brief the person appointed to entertain him during the first two hours of his visit.

"He's in a bad mood, Alan," he told me in Spanish. "He's pissed off with so much waiting around and suspicious about us arriving at nightfall. I think he's texting his boss now."

"Ah, so he does have a boss. That's good to know."

"Why?"

"Er, I'm not sure yet, but please tell Malcolm that."

"OK, Al."

"Please stick to Alan, Arturo."

"OK, Al-an."

I strolled over feeling none too convinced that our fairly flexible plan would work, and when I met the tall, stocky man of forty I feared it was doomed to failure. He looked like one of those EU officials who keep telling us to get our finger out over this Brexit business, and spoke in similarly flat English tones.

"Good evening. I am Arjen," he droned, his pale, plain face practically expressionless.

"Hello there, I'm Alan and I'm going to be showing you around," I chirruped as he shook my hand firmly.

"Where is the owner?"

"Er…" I scratched my head and grinned inanely. I'd been told to feign awkwardness, something which came quite easily to me. "He's a bit busy right now."

He frowned. "How so?"

"Well, er… some other possible buyers have turned up unexpectedly. They were supposed to come on Monday, you see, but their ferry arrived from Mallorca yesterday, and here they are, ha ha." I cringed and rubbed my hands together. "Still, I can give you a tour until Malcolm's free."

He pointed at the Hymer. "Did they come from Mallorca in that?"

"Yes, they were looking at a few places for their commune in the Balearic Islands, but didn't find anywhere suitable."

"A commune?"

I sniggered. "Yes, that's what they say, and you'll see why when you meet them." Although we were alone outside, I moved a little closer to his left ear. "If you ask me, they're wasting Malcolm's time, as I doubt they can afford this place, but he seems to think they can." I shrugged. "Still, you were here first, so if you meet his price it'll be yours, as he's an honourable man, deep down," I said, before warning myself not to overdo the ad-libbing, as my instructions had been crystal clear. I was a mere flunky who would answer his questions concisely and not, Malcolm had insisted, start spouting my usual gibberish and bugger things up.

The man folded his arms and came very near to sneering. "I've made several acquisitions for my organisation and I'm not unfamiliar with the unexpected appearance of rival purchasers."

He lifted his left leg and shook his foot. "So, as you English say." He changed feet and shook the right one. "Pull the other one, because it has bells upon it."

I laughed heartily and even ventured a pat on the arm. "Oh, very good, Ar... Arv..."

"Arjen."

"Very good, Arjen." Like the skilled diplomat I fancied myself to be at that moment in time, the hilarity left my face in an instant. "But I took their call yesterday. They were nearby and wanted to come, and on consulting Malcolm he said we mustn't delay them." I shrugged. "He's generally a good judge of character, but in this case I think he may have, er... erred."

"Are we to spend the whole evening out here?"

"Ha, no, no. Let me get your bags. We've prepared the seco... the best suite for you, yes, the best suite."

While gabbling away as we strolled through the foyer I ignored the minion at the reception desk, but she didn't ignore me. Inma's stern look conveyed the clear message that I ought to pipe down and just do as I'd been told, so after accompanying him to the second best suite, I invited him to take his time freshening up and to meet me in the lounge.

"I need no freshening up. Please show me around now. I may well wish to return to Elda this evening."

"Oh, but we're preparing a special dinner for you... and the Belgians, with the best wines from the cellar."

"I drink no alcohol. Belgians, you say?"

"Yes."

He wrinkled his nose. "French or Flemish speakers?"

"Flemish, I think, though they speak French too, and several other languages." I scratched my chin and looked puzzled. "Come to think of it, they don't seem like your typical hippies at all." I shrugged. "Maybe their lives were very different before."

"Maybe so. Did they drive from Belgium in the Hymer?"

"Yes…" Luckily I noticed his brows rise a millimetre or so. "That's to say, they drove to Spain in a car they brought for some friends from Antwerp who now live in Javea, then bought the Hymer… somewhere on the coast, I believe, before catching the ferry to Mallorca."

"An unusual thing to do."

"Is it?"

"Yes, I believe that even in Belgium there are one or two Hymer dealerships."

I got myself out of that one by telling him that as they were sure to set up their commune somewhere in Spain, they'd decided to buy the vehicle here.

"I see. Anyway, enough about them. Please show me around."

As we flitted from room to room with the master key he made no disparaging noises. On passing the best suite I switched sides to obscure the door and asked him if he thought the layout would be suitable for the proposed sanatorium.

"Possibly." He stopped. "And this room?"

"Oh, the bes… second best suite. The Belgians have that one. It's almost identical to yours, but with… different views."

"I see."

"We'll go back down to the lounge now, then see the rest of the ground floor, unless you'd like a break."

He almost snorted. "A break from what? I wish to see Malcolm right away."

"Right, yes, well, I'll try to arrange that."

He snorted. "Where is he?"

Malcolm had promised to keep Nina and Lars out of his way, in order to spring them upon him shortly before dinner, and on darting off to peer out of a landing window I saw rays of light among the cluster of scrubby pine trees.

"I think they're taking the air," I said loudly.

"In the dark?" he said quietly, his head almost nestling on my shoulder. "What on earth are they doing over there? Have they come to buy the hotel or waste everybody's time?"

As my quick-fire reaction to his Hymer ruse had worked out so well, I began to speak with similarly assured fluency and by the time I'd finishing spinning another yarn I feared I might have gone too far.

He leant on the windowsill and kneaded his brow. "They want to build *what*?"

"A circle of standing stones, among the trees, or maybe around them. I believe it's a, er... druid-type thing which they think will go down well with the commun...ards."

He sniffed and shook his head. "I don't quite believe this is happening to me."

"Ha, yes, it is rather peculiar, isn't it?"

"I came here in the hope of purchasing the hotel and spending the rest of the weekend relaxing in Alicante, and here we are, on Saturday evening, watching some Belgian fools planning a ring of stupid standing stones, in the dark."

"It looks like they're using the torches on their phones," I said helpfully.

He regarded me in a distinctly unfriendly manner. "Then call your boss on his and tell him that I wish to speak to him this instant."

"Er, OK, Arvid. Oops, I mean Ar... Arl..."

"Arjen!"

"Arjen, yes, Arjen, Arjen, I've got it now."

He then took the liberty of jabbing a finger lightly into my chest. "If you ask me, this is a load of bullshit designed to..." He shook his head. "I don't even know what it's designed to achieve. If he doesn't want to sell me the fucking hotel, why not just say so?" He now seemed more like one of those pugnacious Dutch football managers than an EU official.

I tried to look suitably meek and repentant, feeling that the standing stones might have tipped him over the edge. "I'll call him right away," I mumbled.

"You do that. And now I am going to freshen up and reflect on this pathetic charade. Tell the gypsy that he may be driving me to Elda very soon."

"He's only half gypsy."

He growled and stomped away.

I strolled to the stairs, trotted down them and was hotfooting it to the door when Inma stepped into my flight path.

I screeched to a halt on the shiny tiles. "No time now, dear. Oh, hang on though. I told him they want to build a ring of standing stones down by the pines. Pass it on." By means of a deft bit of footwork I escaped her clutches and was soon among the trees, where I found Malcolm, Nina and Lars seated around a picnic table, evidently enjoying themselves despite the chilly breeze.

"I dunno, Lars," said Malcolm. "How do the Dutch riot police disperse a crowd?"

"They shake a church collection box."

"Ha, another good one." He glanced up at me. "What are you panting for? Don't tell me you've driven the bugger away already."

"No, but he's getting impatient. Er, I'm afraid I was forced to make up a story about them wanting to make a ring of standing stones."

He shone his torch in my face. "How the hell did that daft idea come up?"

I shrugged. "I can't remember what he said now, but at the time it seemed like a good response."

"Strewth."

"That's a fine idea, Alan," said Lars, his frizzy locks wilder than ever, due to a spell of radical hair-drying, Nina told me later. "That's just the sort of thing we'd think of. Hey, we could really create one on our land, maybe with great chunks of marble from the abandoned quarries."

Nina squeezed his arm. "Don't get carried away, Lars."

Malcolm stood up. "Right, I'll get to work on the big Dutch berk, but you two had better stay out of the way for a while longer. Either that or sneak up to your room."

Lars nodded pensively, then clicked his fingers. "Alan, could you bring about a dozen chairs outside the main entrance?"

"Er, what for?"

He grinned. "Just put them in a circle, well-spaced out, and leave the rest to us."

"All right."

Malcolm gently tweaked my ear. "Anything else to report, chatterbox?"

I summarised my prattling and the Dutchman's responses. "So he's a bit sceptical about the whole thing right now."

"Who wouldn't be? That's just how we want him. So, Lars, are you planning a little shindig?"

"Yes, I feel we must capitalise on the standing stones story. Alan can tell you when to bring him to a window."

"OK, Lars." He cackled. "I haven't enjoyed myself so much since I loosed a load of rats in a competitor's warehouse, but that was donkey's years ago."

"Yes, it's great fun," I said. "But I'm not sure it's the best way to make him buy. I think he's reaching the end of his tether."

"Oh, who cares? I'll sell it soon anyway, and don't worry, you'll get your slice. Right, let's go on making memories." As he faded into the darkness, chuckling softly, I realised he was still wearing his shiny tracksuit.

About half an hour later, by means of a nod here and a wink there, Malcolm steered his prey to the largest window in the lounge, from where he was privileged to observe Nina, Lars and Arturo dancing around the chair circle I'd recently constructed. The couple favoured a Red Indian-style circumnavigation, involving sundry whoops and appeals to the heavens, while Arturo shuffled along in their wake, twirling his arms and clicking his fingers in a distinctly flamenco-esque manner.

"This is becoming utterly ridiculous," Inma said to me from the small reception window.

"I know, but Malcolm's enjoying himself, which is the main thing."

"Not to me, it isn't."

I tried to explain that his gratitude to us for having helped to engineer this remarkable evening would undoubtedly be rewarded at some time in the not too distant future.

She grunted. "I came here to make twenty thousand, or at least ten."

I tutted. "Don't be greedy, dear. It doesn't become you."

She sighed. "Recent developments suggest that we may need that extra money."

"Oh."

"I'd better see how Randi and the others are getting along in the kitchen."

"OK." She strode away. "Arrrgh!" I cried, or a noise very much to that effect. "Randi! Arvid! Of course, it's their house you want us to buy!"

She spun around and clapped her fingers lightly. "Well done, Sherlock. It's about time you guessed. Now you can set about messing that up too."

I pointed towards the window. "But... but I didn't make them dance around like idiots."

She frowned. "No, but you made up that ridiculous standing stones story."

I held up my hands. "Guilty as charged, but I promise not so say a word to Randi or Arjen, I mean Arvid."

"Stay out of the kitchen."

"Sí, cariño."

When the dancers had tired themselves out I was privileged to be present at their meeting with the Dutchman, from which Malcolm had absented himself for reasons unbeknownst to me. As Nina hadn't yet donned her jewellery she looked like a fairly standard ageing hippy lady, but in the clear lights of the lounge and without his coat I saw that Lars had really excelled himself, as follows, from the bottom up: dusty sandals, odd socks, yellow and black stripy trousers with leather patches on the knees, a knotted rope for a belt, a ragged Greenpeace t-shirt, and the same colourfully embroidered waistcoat he'd been wearing when we'd first met.

What really took old Arjen aback, however, was Lars' astonishingly good English as he made the sort of small-talk you'd expect from the sound bourgeois folk they undoubtedly were. After asking him about his trip from Holland, he apologised profusely for having coincided with him at the hotel.

"I think the owner's peculiarly English sense of humour has made him wish to throw us together, goodness knows why."

"Yes," Arjen mouthed, but no sound emerged.

"But rest assured that despite our interest in the property, we won't interfere with your negotiations. Should you decide not to buy, tomorrow we may well make a bid of our own, though I shouldn't think we'll go quite as high as eight-hundred thousand."

"No," he managed to utter.

Lars chortled. "We're not made of money, after all."

"It is a charming little place though," Nina chipped in.

"Yes, it is. Come along, dear. I need to tidy myself up a little before dinner." He bowed to the stunned Dutchman, Nina took his arm, and he escorted her up the stairs like an ambassador leaving the presence of his sovereign.

I sighed. "I just can't make them out. Can you?"

"This is all a lot of infantile play-acting."

"Yes, I don't think they're quite right in the head."

"Hmm, I'm not so sure about that."

"I expect they'll buzz off in their Hymer tomorrow and go and annoy someone else. If I were you I wouldn't worry about them, Ar...jen."

When his phone pinged he gave a start. "When will dinner begin?"

"In about half an hour."

He hurried up the stairs, phone in hand.

As you've already seen, Lars was full of surprises, so when he appeared in a pristine dinner jacket, impeccably pressed trousers and shiny black shoes even I was struck dumb, partly due to the way his fluorescent bow-tie made a mockery of the rest of his getup. Nina had changed too, into a plain but elegant blue dress, stylish medium-heeled shoes, and no jewellery at all, apart from her sparkling tiara which no longer looked quite so incongruous. Not only did Arjen suspect its authenticity right away, but he soon asked permission to handle the gem-laden band.

He smiled dreamily as he held it at different angles to the light. "It's a beautiful tiara. My uncle is a jeweller in Amsterdam and he taught me quite a lot about the business when I was younger. I think this was made in the nineteenth century, possibly in England, judging by the style of the chevrons. Am I right?"

"Yes, I believe my great-great-grandfather bought it in London at the time of Queen Victoria's golden jubilee. He was a young diplomat at the time, about to be married." She tittered. "Due to the lifestyle we've chosen I seldom wear it, so tonight, in more refined company, I decided to take the opportunity."

Arjen smiled and even coloured slightly, clearly impressed by her pedigree, before asking them about their life before coming to Spain. After hearing about their successful careers he became curious enough to ask them why they'd chosen their current modus vivendi. Lars then rambled on at length about breaking with the past and releasing one's creative impulses, and Malcolm soon began to look a little bored. He'd finally changed into smart casual clothes and only opened his mouth to eat Randi's delicious fiskeboller (Norwegian-style fish balls) followed by a divine dish of fårikål (mutton and cabbage stew) served by Inma and Rosa who both wore pretty aprons and pretended to find the Dutchman attractive by means of coy little smiles and a bit of eyelash fluttering. I, of course, had been told to keep my trap firmly shut unless Arjen addressed me directly.

"We're mere dilettantes, you see," Lars went on. "Amusing ourselves with our artistic endeavours and spending time with like-minded folk." He chuckled. "Our proposed commune will be an attempt to bring together an extended group of friends and acquaintances from all over Europe. We hope to generate a lot of creative energy, and who knows, some of us may eventually produce something worthwhile."

"Very interesting," said Arjen, looking more relaxed than I'd seen him up to then.

Randi had only managed to bake a few sirupsnippers (spiced biscuits) for dessert, so coffee was served at the same time. Arjen asked them about the proposed standing stones and fortunately Lars was able to back up my fantasy with some convincing chatter about sourcing the marble, transport logistics and so forth, proving yet again that my brainwaves emerge from the recesses of a deep and resourceful mind, perhaps. The guest of honour had just polished off his second sirupsnipper when Malcolm rose to his feet.

"It's time for you and me to have a chat, Arjen," he said, his deep voice slightly mellower than usual.

"Yes, Malcolm."

After instructing me to have more coffee sent into the adjoining sitting room, he showed the Dutchman out and winked at us before softly closing the door behind him.

When Inma came in I ordered her to serve more coffee to the men.

"Don't talk to me like that," she muttered. "So how is it going?"

"It's too soon to say. Get back to the kitchen," I said, before sending her away with a firm pat on the bum. "For once I have her at my beck and call," I explained to Nina and Lars.

"Ha!" said my wife, before toddling off.

An hour later we began to feel sleepy. I'd put my ear to the door a few time, but had only discerned a low rumble emanating from Malcolm's diaphragm, so Nina suggested turning in.

"I'm sure they'll strike a deal eventually, and it may well be advantageous to Malcolm, so perhaps we ought not to be around when they finish."

Lars smiled and smoothed back his still startling hair. "Yes, on seeing us again our Dutch friend might experience a moment of lucidity and realise that he's had his arm twisted in a most cunning way, so we'd better retire."

After accompanying them to the foot of the stairs I repaired to the kitchen, where I found Inma and Arturo emptying the industrial dishwasher, the others having already gone home. I suddenly remembered a trifling matter which had slipped my mind during the crucial dinner party.

"The Norwegians' house, eh?"

She tossed me a dish towel. "Yes, if you like it."

"Hmm, well, I shall have to sleep on it, possibly for several nights." I deftly dried a bowl. "Fortunately Arvid never got round to those ridiculous modifications he once planned, so let me see. Hmm, it is an airy house with that nice conservatory, the pool, and a not overlarge vegetable plot that I can get stuck into."

"And solar panels on the garage roof."

"Ooh, yes, I'd forgotten about those, and then of course the garage underneath them will... would come in handy."

She smiled. "You could make it into a music room, or a photography workshop."

I remembered my square foot of collage, still on the bedspread. "Ah, well..."

"And as Liz will be quite close by you can begin those keyboard and singing classes you once proposed."

"Yes, that might motivate me again. Would the conservatory be a good place for you to paint?"

"Yes, apart from in summer. Randi says they'll leave the blinds in there, assuming we come to an agreement with her husband. They've decided to return to the same place in Norway. Randi has already been offered her old job and as Arvid works online it makes no difference to him."

"Who's the main instigator?"

"Randi. She likes it well enough here, but she misses her family and friends, and the ingredients she likes to cook with. By promising him lengthy winter holidays, so he can keep up his cycling, she's convinced him that it's best to go back." She frowned. "The trouble is, he insists on getting €200,000 for the house."

I dropped the dish towel. "That's too much for us, and for anyone else, I think. He needs to be convinced that he'll never get so much for it, or not for a long time." I picked up the towel and promptly dropped it again. "Hey, and he only paid Ken about €160,000 for it, the greedy devil."

She sighed. "I hoped he'd accept €180,000, but he's being very stubborn."

I then pictured the house in the olive grove which Juanca and I had walked to. "There are plenty of excellent houses in that price range, so we've no reason to buy theirs."

"Isn't that place near your sister's?" said Arturo.

I nodded.

"Well, you should buy it then. Family is the most important thing in the world, Alan, and one must try to stay as close as possible to them. Besides, Bernie's a great guy and your sister's nice too. Yes, you must pressure that skinflint to lower the price and make the house yours."

I recalled Juanca's words about the rootlessness of the English. I pictured his cheeky face, then Arvid's impassive one. I gasped. "Arvid needs to be wankered!" I cried in English.

They both gazed at me.

"Perdona. I'll send Juanca round to see him right away."

Inma wrinkled her cute little nose, still powdered with a little sirupsnipper dust. "What good will that do?"

"Oh, he'll easily convince him that he'll never get that price for the place, somehow."

Inma folded her dishcloth and placed it on the stainless steel top. "I have an even better idea."

"Go on."

She cleared her throat. "Arvid will not only be wankered, but he will also be Malcolmed," she said in English. "At the same time," she concluded in Spanish.

"Hmm."

Arturo clicked his fingers. "Hey, how about if I go with some of my rough gypsy friends? Maybe they can scare him into selling it to you really cheap."

"A nice thought, but no thanks," I said. "So, a joint assault by Juanca and Malcolm, you think?"

"Yes, Juanca could take him there and Malcolm... would know what to do."

"Malc's going home soon."

I nodded. "Yes, and we don't even know if he's going to pull off this deal yet. If we don't get a slice of the pie, even one-eighty will be too much."

Inma smiled. "We can manage that amount without any... windfall from this place."

"Can we?"

"Of course. I believe our solar sales will rise some more, then gradually fall to a constant level which will provide us with a good income for a long time to come, and with much less effort than we're making now. We can just about pay for the house, then gradually replenish our bank account, and the cornflakes box."

"Ooh, we never did look at the post-its with our predictions for the end of last month."

"I threw them away. They became irrelevant after Bernie and I joined the team."

"True."

"Can I sell panels too?" said Arturo.

I managed not to chuckle. "Er, well, you see–"

"Yes, you could take some leaflets and have a go, if you like."

"Gracias." He glared at me. Some gypsies have plenty of money, you know, Alan."

"Yes, I'm sure they have."

He grinned. "And they like shiny things, but they won't buy from a payo, so I guess I'll soon be putting my rings back on. This Dutch guy's just a lackey, so I doubt there'll be a job for me here."

I looked at my watch. "He might not buy."

"Want to bet? I know Malc better than you by now and a hundred euros says the guy will buy."

"Alan never bets more than a euro, Arturo."

"I won't bet anyway. I also think the guy will buy."

As we were putting away the final plates we heard voices from the foyer. I took a couple of steps in that direction.

"Whoa!" said Arturo. "Give the poor guy chance to get to his room."

The door swung open and Malcolm began to survey the sparkling surfaces. "Any more of them tasty bickies left?"

Inma took a plateful from the fridge and removed the cling-film.

"Ta, love." He munched, sighed, then munched some more. After wiping the crumbs from his mouth he finally looked at us. "Well, that's done and dusted, but it was a close call. He wanted to sign in the morning, but I thought his subconscious might get to work and he'd wake up having second thoughts, so I settled for what he'd offered and we put pen to paper just now. It's only a rough contract, but he knows that if he goes back on it I'll chop his balls off." He sighed. "Ah, it was good fun while it lasted."

"De puta madre," said Arturo, a very crude way of saying 'great'.

"Yes, it was fun," said Inma.

"A memory to cherish," said I.

"€765,000," said Malcolm. "With just sixty five in cash, so that's fifteen for you two and a bit of loose change for me, ha ha."

I rubbed my hands together.

"Ten thousand for us, and five will be divided among our... accomplices," said Inma, taking the words right out of my mouth, give or take a couple of thousand.

"De puta madre," said Arturo, beginning to count on his ringless fingers.

14

I'll buck the trend in this book and not attempt to end with a bang as I usually do, although the aftermath of the hotel saga was unremarkable in most respects.

We drove home that night, but Lars later told me that over breakfast the Dutchman had seemed happy enough with the deal. He'd asked them to stay in touch and let him know where they finally set up their commune, even hinting that he might pay them a visit, were he to find himself nearby. Malcolm was good enough to get us the cash before flying home, and in return I promised to try to sell the Hymer for him, with my brother-in-law's invaluable assistance, of course. Bernie felt sorely tempted to buy it himself, but Cathy convinced him that Malcolm's modest price tag – €60,000 for a vehicle which had cost him over a hundred – was far too much for a budding farmer to pay, and just think of the land he could buy for that amount.

"So I've definitely got my eye on this field now," he said to me one sunny mid-March day. "Or we could make the bloke an offer between us."

"Alas, the almond trees are in blossom, but our bank account is bare," I said, as Arvid had held out for €190,000, unimpressed by Juanca's scathing assessment of the property, though I doubt even Malcolm could have budged the obstinate beggar.

"Oh well, you'll be moving in soon, and the panel money's pouring in, so there'll be time enough to think about twisting the bloke's arm." He sighed. "I bet he won't sell though. He's a proper farmer like me and won't part with an inch of land." He glanced over at the Hymer. "Oh, I'd better flog that bloody thing before I start seeing my name on it."

"Malcolm says we can take a trip in it if we like, but I'd be scared of scratching it."

"Yeah, like last time, you big wuss. You know, when you go up north I think we'd like to come with you."

"Be our guests, or Juanje's guests. I'm sure he won't mind putting you up." I gazed over at our future home which Randi and Arvid were about to vacate. "Ah, it's going to feel like a whole new era living over here again. Once our solar crusade calms down Inma's going to get into her painting and I've spoken to Liz about having singing classes up at our dear, dingy old cave house, and maybe keyboard classes too, though to be honest I can't see myself playing Rachmaninov anytime soon."

"And what about that funny photography lark you were on with?"

"Oh, I don't know. Lars and Nina are only ten minutes away, so I'll probably seek inspiration there. Perhaps I'll collaborate with them and they'll help to get my creative juices flowing."

"Ugh!"

"They really are going to build a ring of standing stones, you know, and that's down to my bright idea. He's been driving round the old marble quarries and looking into haulage and things." I shook my head. "Ah, the things people do to make life more interesting."

"Pair of loonies, if you ask me. Oh, how's old Zefe getting on?"

"Álvaro tells me that theirs is still a harmonious household. He feared that the old devil would remind him of his generous gift every day, but instead he just demands to be taken for drives all the time, which suits him fine, as he's so chuffed to have a new car at last. I'm sure we'll be seeing them over here before long."

"Hmm, so is there no sign of old Zefe weakening?"

"No, Bernie."

"Ah, I still look at photos of that Sierra Pelada now and then. I reckon that after a month there he ought to have made at least–"

"And another oldie who's thriving is Jesús," I interrupted, wishing to prevent another outbreak of gold fever. "His panels are now the talk of the bar, mainly because he talks about them all the time. Vicente tells me that a couple of blokes are thinking of buying much bigger setups just to shut him up, so we can expect a few orders from there, touch wood," I said, as we'd become a true team by then, sharing in each other's successes.

"That's good. Ah, pretty soon we'll have the whole area wrapped up, then we'll mostly just sit back and wait for folk to call us."

"Yes, then I'll nip down to the bar and don my apron. I do think I could make a few sales though, given the chance."

He smiled. "Leave that to us, mate. Do a bit of coin dealing, lend a hand at the bar, and work on your singing. You aren't bad you know, and it might lead somewhere one day."

I gasped. "Do you really think I might be able to… perform… in front of… people?"

"You might, if you put your mind to it." He stood up. "Come on, it's about time you learnt how to plough with Spartacus."

I leapt to my feet. "Oh, so many new things to do! Can't life be wonderful if you make all the right decisions, Bern?"

"Yes, Alan, it sure can."

To be continued, possibly under a slightly different title...

Printed in Great Britain
by Amazon

33421711R00123